Magic and Magical Fetish

Magic and Magical Fetish
Author: Alfred C. Haddon

Original title: *Magic and Fetishism* (1906)
Cover image: *Shaumonekusse, Prairie Wolf* (c. 1822), Charles Bird King
Lay-out: www.burokd.nl

ISBN 978-94-92355-30-0

© 2017 Revised publication by:

VAMzzz Publishing
P.O. Box 3340
1001 AC Amsterdam
The Netherlands
www.vamzzz.com
contactvamzzz@gmail.com

MAGIC AND
MAGICAL FETISH

Alfred C. Haddon

VAMzzz PUBLISHING

Alfred Cort Haddon, Sc.D., FRS, FRGS
Finsbury, 24 May 1855 – Cambridge, 20 April 1940

contents

Prefatory Note

It is by no means easy to do justice to such a large, comprehensive, and at the same time vague subject as magic in the small compass of a Primer, and part of even that small space had to be devoted to another subject. For sins of omission I must claim this excuse; for sins of commission I claim the indulgence of the reader.

A. C. H.

MAGIC

I. Sympathetic Magic

AS KNOWLEDGE INCREASES, mankind learns more and more about the world and the processes of nature, but even at the present day the vast majority of white men possess only a rudimentary amount of this knowledge; indeed, most so-called educated people have very vague ideas concerning the physical universe in which they live. Such being the case, it is not surprising that primitive peoples have very confused notions concerning these matters, and, as the result of false inductions concerning the causes of phenomena, they seek to accomplish ends by means that we recognize as inadequate. 'It is plain', as Dr. Jevons points out [36, 33], 'that as long as man is turned loose as it were amongst these innumerable possible causes with nothing to guide his choice, the chances against his making the right selection are considerable.' Further, 'no progress could be made in science until man had distinguished, at any rate roughly, possible from absolutely impossible effects (or causes), and had learned to dismiss from consideration the impossible. It might be expected that the experience would suffice of itself to teach man this essential distinction, but the vast majority of the human race has not yet learned from experience that like does not necessarily produce like: four-fifths of mankind, probably, believe in sympathetic magic'.

The instances of sympathetic magic as Dr. Him points out [32, 278] are naturally divided into two main classes which, broadly speaking, correspond to the two types of association, contiguity and similarity, and as in psychology it is often difficult to decide whether a given associative process has its origin in a relation of contiguity or in one of similarity, so it is often an open question to which group a given superstition is to be assigned. We will start from the facts that are simpler and easier to explain.

A. CONTAGIOUS MAGIC

Hair, nail-pairings, etc. — scalp-lock — saliva — luck-ball — foot-prints — clothes — rag bushes and pin-wells — personal 'ornaments' — food — cannibalism — sympathetic relations between persons — couvade

Sympathetic Magic based on a material connection between things [32, 279] has been aptly termed by Dr. Frazer [21, 77] Contagious Magic. All over the world we meet with examples of the belief that objects which were once related to one another retain their connection, though they may be separated, and whatever may happen to one part or object the other part or object is similarly affected; thus, by acting upon a part of a given whole we may influence the whole as well as all its other parts.

This belief explains why a magician, wishing to influence or act upon some particular individual, desires to obtain some portion of his body or something actually connected with him. A few hairs from the beard, a lock of hair, some nail-parings, a drop of blood from the nose, which has fallen to the ground, and which has not been rendered impalpable by effacing it with the foot, are used by Basuto sorcerers [10, 277], and indeed by workers of magic everywhere. A few of the examples collected by Mr. Hartland [30, ii. 66] will suffice to demonstrate the universality of this belief. In some parts of England a girl forsaken by her lover is advised to get a lock of his hair and boil it; whilst it is simmering in the pot he will have no rest. In certain parts of Germany and Transylvania the clippings of the hair or nails, as well as broken pieces of the teeth, are buried beneath the elder tree which grows in the courtyard, or are burnt, or carefully hidden, for fear of witches. Patagonians burn the hairs brushed out from their heads, and all the parings of their nails, for they believe that spells may be wrought upon them by anyone who can obtain a piece of either.

The potency of the hair is shown in the beliefs about the long, narrow beaded band which is used to tie up the hair of a Musquakie woman [56, 96, 7]. This, though a talisman when first worn, becomes something infinitely more sacred and precious, being transfused with the essence of her soul; any one gaining possession of it has her for an abject slave if he keeps it, and kills her if he destroys it. A woman will go from a man she loves to a man she hates if he has contrived to possess himself of her hair-string; and a man will forsake wife and children for a witch who has touched his lips with her hair-string.

The hair-string is made for a girl by her mother or grandmother and decorated with luck 'patterns'; it is also prayed over by the maker and a shaman. The scalp-lock ornament worn by the Musquakie men is kept with great care as it helps to protect the soul. As the tearing out of the scalp-lock makes the soul at its root the slave of the one obtaining it, so the possession of its ornament and shield, which has absorbed some of its essence, gives the possessor the ability to send the rightful owner brain fever and madness [56, 106].

In the South Sea Islands it was necessary to the success of any sorcery to secure something connected with the body of the victim. Accordingly a spittoon was always carried by the confidential servant of a chief in the Hawaiian Islands to receive his expectorations, which were carefully buried every morning. The Tahitians used to burn or bury the hair they cut off, and every individual among them had his distinct basket for food. As Mr. Hartland points out [30, ii. 76], the custom, everywhere practised, of obliterating all trace of the saliva after spitting, doubtless originated in the desire to prevent the use of it for magical purposes, and the same desire led to the extreme cleanliness in the disposal of fouler excreta which is almost universally a characteristic of savages. Thus, this belief has been one of the most beneficial of superstitions.

Luck-bags of red cloth, which contain 'the four things of good fortune', are made by witches in Italy [43, 287], who while sewing it sing an incantation. American Negroes brought over from West Africa the art of making *luck-balls* or *cunjerin bags*, a practice which is kept up to the present day. They are supposed to bring happiness and success in everything the owner undertakes; one made for Charles G. Leland, at the instigation of Miss Owen [57, 173], contained, in addition to knotted threads, a piece of foil to represent the brightness of the little spirit that was going to be in the ball, a leaf of clover *in the place of the hair of the one that is going to own the ball*, and some dust which was designed to blind the eyes of enemies. Miss Owen got the same man, Alexander, the King of the Voodoos, who made the ball for Mr. Leland, to make one for me, and she informed me that 'it was made just like Mr. Leland's with the same words and with the same materials, excepting the clover. This is not the season for clover, *so a fragment of paper, torn from one of your books, represents you.*'

It is not essential that the object to be operated upon should have formed an actual part of a person, for something associated with that person, such as something habitually worn or used, is sufficient, or as in the case of the luck-ball just cited, the association may be as remote as that between an author and a piece of the paper of a book he has published.

Earth from a man's footprints, on account of its close contact with the person, has acquired the virtues of a portion of his body. Widely spread in Germany is the belief that if a sod whereon a man has trodden—all the better if with the naked foot—be taken up and dried behind the hearth or oven, he will parch up with it and lan-guish, or his foot will be withered. He will be lamed, or even killed, by sticking his footprint with nails—coffin nails are the best—or broken glass [30, ii. 78]; but these are also the practices of Australian or other savages. To quote only one example from Australia [34, 26], sharp fragments of quartz, glass, bone, or charcoal are buried in the footprints of the victim or in the mark made in the ground by his reclining body. They are supposed to enter the victim, and rheumatic affections are very frequently attributed to them.

Clothes, from their intimate association with the person, have naturally attained a prominent place among the instruments of witchcraft. In Germany and Denmark no portion of a survivor's clothing must on any account be put upon a corpse, else the owner will languish away as it moulders in the grave. To hang rags from the clothing of a dead man upon a vine is to render it barren. 'Probably, as Mr. Hartland suggests, it is only a different interpretation of the same belief which alike in Christian, in Mohammedan, and in Buddhist lands has led to the ascription of marvellous powers to the clothes and other relics of departed saints. The divine power which was immanent in these personages during life attaches not merely to every portion of their bodies, but to every shred of their apparel' [30, ii. 90]. An illustrative parallel can be taken from the Pacific. The red feathers, which adorned the sacred girdle worn by the Tahitian kings were taken from the images of the gods. The girdle: thus became sacred, even as the person of the gods, the feathers being supposed to retain all the dreadful attributes of power and vengeance which the idols possessed, and with which it was designed to endow the king.' So potent was it that Mr. Ellis says [17, iii. 108] it 'not only raised him to the highest earthly station, but identified him with their gods.'

It is conceivable, as Mr. Hartland suggests [30, ii. 214], that unedu-
cated folks might argue thus: if an article of my clothing in a witch's
hands may cause me to suffer, the same article in contact with a
beneficent power may relieve pain, restore me to health, or promote
my general prosperity. Hence the practice of throwing pins into
wells, of tying rags on bushes and trees, of driving nails into trees
and stocks, of throwing stones and sticks on cairns, and the analogous practices throughout the world, suggest that they are to be
interpreted as acts of ceremonial union with the spirit identified with
well, tree, stock, or cairn [30, ii. 228]. In the British Islands the sanctity
of the well or bush was subsequently annexed by the missionaries
who took up their abode beside them, and thus we find the wells or
trees called after certain saints and the healing power attributed to
the latter, whereas the holiness and efficacy of the wells were in the
vast majority of cases, if not in all, pre-Christian [27, 383].

Objects are worn or eaten so that by induction the individual may acquire their properties. Thus the Red Indian hunter [70, 131]
wears ornaments of the claws of the grizzly bear, that he may be
endowed with its courage and ferocity, and the Tyrolese hunter still
wears tufts of eagle's down in his hat, to gain the eagle's keen sight
and courage. 'Look,' writes Casalis [10, 271], 'at those strange objects
hanging from the necks of our little black friends. There is a kite's
foot in order that the poor child may escape misfortune with the
swiftness of the kite in its flight. Another has the claw of a lion in
order that his life may be as firmly secured against all danger as
that of a lion; a third is adorned with the tarsus bone of a sheep, or

an iron ring, that he may oppose to evil a resistance as firm as iron, or as that little compact bone without marrow which could not be crushed between two stones without difficulty.'

The eating of certain kinds of food, more especially of the flesh of animals, would similarly have a very potent effect; thus among the Dyaks [65, i. 176], young men sometimes abstain from eating the flesh of deer, lest they should become timid. The Abipones of Paraguay [14, 258] 'detest the thought of eating hens, eggs, sheep, fish, or tortoises, imagining that these tender kinds of food engender sloth and languor in their bodies and cowardice in their minds. On the other hand, they eagerly devour the flesh of the tiger [jaguar], bull, stag, boar, anta and tamandua [anteaters], having an idea that, from continually feeding on these animals, their strength, boldness, and courage are increased.'

Belief in contagious magic leads quite logically to various revolting practices. In Torres Straits the sweat of renowned warriors was drunk by young men, who also ate mixed with their food the scrapings from the fingernails of the warriors which had become saturated with human blood in order 'to make strong and like a stone; no afraid' [29, v. 301]. The eyes and tongue of a freshly killed enemy were frequently torn out and given to lads to make them brave and fearless. The Australian natives believe that a man's fat and his strength and vitality are connected, therefore the wasting of the body and disease are the result of the absence of fat, perhaps to be followed by death. By eating a man's fat, and thus making it part of himself, the black fellow thinks that he also acquires the strength of the deceased. So also they think that human fat brings success in hunting, causes spears which are anointed with it to fly true, or the club to strike irresistible blows. The possession of human fat is, therefore, much desired by these aborigines, especially those who feel age or disease, or who wish to be successful in the magical arts, for it is believed that the spirit of the dead man whose fat has been used will help the charm to act [35, 411, 361]. Cannibalism for magical purposes of this sort has probably been extremely common and is possibly at the base of a good deal of anthropophagy.

Very widely spread is the belief that close relatives or even friends are bound together in a sympathetic relation, which is especially manifest on important occasions or at critical times. When a Land Dyak village has turned out for a wild-pig hunt in the jungle, those who remain at home may not touch water or oil with their hands during the absence of their friends, lest the hunters should all become 'butterfingered,' and the prey so escape them [60, i. 430]. It is also recorded from Borneo that when men are on a war expedition, fires are lighted at home, the mats are spread, and the fires kept up till late in the evening and lighted again before dawn, so that the men may not be cold; the roofing of the house is opened before dawn, so that the men may not lie too long and so fall into the enemies' hands [60, ii. 104]. Again, when a Dyak is out headhunting, his wife, or, if he is unmarried, his sister, must wear a sword day and night, in order that he may be always thinking of his weapons; and she may not sleep during the day nor go to bed before two in the morning, lest her husband or brother should thereby be surprised in his sleep by an enemy [20, l. 30]. Similar instances could easily be multiplied indefinitely from various savage countries, but even in Europe, there are not lacking records of a real sympathy between husband and wife, where the former suffers from certain characteristic ailments of the latter [59, 240]. There is a very widely spread series of customs based upon the belief that the father and his unborn or newly born child are in such sympathetic relationship that the former has to take all sorts of precautions lest his offspring should in any way be injured. The extreme form this custom takes is for the newly made father to take to his bed and be specially dieted; this occurs in many places, but notably in the East Indian Archipelago and in South America. The custom, which is known as the *Couvade*, is subject to many modifications, which have been tabulated and discussed by Mr. H. Ling Roth [59, 204]. Among the Land Dyaks of Borneo the husband of a pregnant woman, until the time of her delivery, may not do work with any sharp instrument, except what may be absolutely necessary for the cultivation of his farm; he may not tie things together with rattans, or strike animals, or fire guns, or do anything of a violent character for fear of injuring the child. Often the men must abstain from certain food lest it should affect the child; thus in Guiana partaking of the Agouti would make the child meagre, or eating a *labba* would make the infant's mouth protrude, like the *labba's*, or make it spotted like the *labba*, which spots would ultimately become ulcers [59, 220]. Thus the father is frequently debarred from performing many of the usual unconsidered daily acts, lest they should affect the welfare of a child that is newly born or is about to be born; and there is the curious development of the belief of an occult reaction of the expected child on the father, affecting, to take one example, his success in fishing [59, 234].

B. HOMŒOPATHIC MAGIC

Plants — rain-making — wind-making — increase of plants, and of animals — luring animals to be caught — human effigies to injure or kill people

When man first began to think about the world around him, he must have noted (what he, in common with other animals, had uncon- sciously acted upon in the past) that day and night and the seasons arrived in regular succession, the same stars rose and set, an animal reproduced its own kind, in fact that there was a uniformity in nature. But side by side with these natural sequences there were irregu- larities. Some days were shorter than others, some were bright, others cloudy, the length and character of the seasons varied from year to year, some stars had a course in the heavens independent of the majority. Again, he might early have noticed that many of these fluctuations in sunshine and rain, in heat and cold, affected him directly or indirectly by influencing vegetation. We need not be surprised, therefore, if he came to the conclusion that it would be better for him if he exerted himself to regulate matters somewhat, but then the difficulty would arise, what was he to do?

The unenlightened mind does not discriminate between cause and effect, and imagines that as like produces like, so a result can be attained by imitating it. Hence arose Mimetic or Symbolic Magic, which, following Dr. Hirn, is better termed Homœopathic Magic, which is occult influence based upon a likeness between things [32, 282]. On this was founded the mediaeval medical theory known as the Doctrine of Signatures, which supposes that plants and minerals indicate by their external characters the diseases which nature intended them to remedy.

It would be easy to give a large number of examples to illustrate homœopathic magic, but a few will suffice. Thus the Euphrasia, or eyebright, was, and is, supposed to be good for the eyes, on the strength of a black pupil-like spot in its corolla [70, 123]. The yellow turmeric, or saffron, cured jaundice. The roots of roses or their slips, with their knots removed and set amongst broom, will bring forth yellow roses [47, x, 70]. The influence of homeopathic magic can be traced in beliefs and practices from the lowest savages to civilized nations. The magician who works by similarities makes representations of things or beings, in order to acquire an influence over them. By dramatic or pictorial imitation heavenly bodies are influenced, rain is made, plants and animals are increased, animals enticed to their destruction, human beings acted upon.

When it was wished to cause rain to fall in Murray Island, Torres Straits, the rain-maker scooped a hole in the ground, and lined it with leaves and placed in it a rude stone image of a man which had previously been anointed with oil and rubbed with scented grass; then he poured the decoction of minced leaves of various plants mixed with water over the image—the image being so laid in the hole as to point to the quarter from which the rain was expected. Earth was heaped over the image and leaves and shells placed on the mound, and all the while the rain-maker muttered an incantation in a low sepulchral tone. Four large screens composed of plaited coconut leaves were placed at the head, foot, and sides of the grave to represent clouds; on the upper part of each was fastened a blackened oblong of vegetable cloth to mimic a black thundercloud, and coconut leaves, with their leaflets pointing downwards, were suspended close by to represent rain. A torch was ignited and waved lengthwise over the grave; the smoke represented clouds and the flames mimicked lightning, and a bamboo clapper was sounded to imitate thunder.

The rain was supposed to come when the decoction round the image was rotten. The incantation consisted of enumerating various aspects of certain forms of clouds. Rain could be made in this manner only by one section of the community, and amongst these one or two men had a much greater reputation than the others [29, vi.]. This may be taken as an example of a typical rainmaking ceremony, in which all the phenomena of a thunder shower are imitated.

If a native of Mabuiag, in Torres Straits, required rain, he went to the rain-maker and asked him to make some. The latter might reply, 'You go and put some more thatch on your house and on mine too'; this was to keep out the forthcoming rain. The rain-maker painted the front of his body white, and the back black. This was explained by my informant thus: 'All along same as clouds, black behind, white he go first,' or he painted his body with black spots to make the clouds come separately; when they congregated, the rain fell. The rain-maker put medicine 'in his right hand and waved it towards his body and chanted an incantation. To stop the rain the rain-maker put red paint on the crown of his head, to represent the shining sun, and ruddled his body all over. He then lay doubled up and was closely surrounded with three mats, so that no wind could penetrate to him. Finally, he burnt some leaves on the seashore close to the water, on a rising tide; the smoke represented the clouds, and as it was dissipated so they disappeared, and as the encroaching sea washed away the ashes, so the clouds were scattered' [29, v. 350].

In the island of Muralug certain old men could raise a wind by very rapidly whirling a thin bullroarer attached to a long string. More wind could be obtained by climbing to the top of a tree and performing there. In this case the noise made by the bull-roarer imitated that produced by a gale of wind [29, v. 352]. Examples of the magical increase of plants are found in the 'yam stones' placed in their gardens by various Papuans, which by their rounded shape suggest the actual tubers [28, 202; 29, vi.].

The following instances are culled from that treasury of folk custom and belief — *The Golden Bough.* In Thüringen the man who sows flax carries the seed in a long bag which reaches from his shoulders to his knees, and he walks with long strides, so that the bag sways to and fro on his back. It is believed that this will cause the flax to wave in the wind. In the interior of Sumatra rice is sown by women who, in sowing, let their hair hang loose down their back, in order that the rice may grow luxuriantly and have long stalks. It is commonly believed in Germany and Austria that leaping high in the fields will make the flax or hemp grow tall. A Bavarian sower, in sowing wheat, will sometimes wear a golden ring, in order that the corn may have a fine yellow colour [20, i. 35, 36].

As references are given on pp. 41-44 to magical practices for the increase of animals, further examples need not be added here, their object being to provide plenty of food for the community. It was for the same reason that images of fish, turtle, and dugong were made by the islanders of Torres Straits and taken with them when they went fishing, with the idea that the image lured the real animal to its destruction; and men of the dugong clan who were symbolically decorated made mimetic movements with a dead dugong to constrain others to come and be caught [29, v. 337, 182, and vi.].

The same people used to carve small human effigies out of thin slabs of wood and coat them with beeswax, or the images were made entirely of beeswax. These figures were treated in various ways for nefarious magic, but always the first action was to call them by the names of the persons who were to be affected by them. If the magician pulled an arm or a leg of the image, the patient felt sore in the corresponding limb, and became ill, and eventually died in great pain; should the magician restore the dismembered limb, the patient would recover. If a magician pricked with the spine of a stingray an image that had been named, the person indicated would be stung in the same place by a sting ray when he went fishing on the reef [29 v.

[324]. Analogous customs are to this day practiced in Britain. The first example comes from Ross-shire [48, 373]. The *corp creagh* is a body of clay rudely shaped into the image of a person whose hurt is desired. After a tolerably correct representation is obtained, it is stuck all over with pins and thorns and placed in a running stream. As the image is worn away by the action of the water the victim also wastes away with some mortal disease. The more pins that are stuck in from time to time the more excruciating agony the victim suffers. Should, however, any wayfarer discover the *corp* in the stream, the spell is broken and the victim duly recovers. From Argyleshire we learn [49, 144] that a long incantation was used as the pins were being put in the clay image, the beginning of which was something to this effect: 'As you waste away, may waste away; as this wounds you, may it wound.' When it was desired that the person should die a lingering death, care was taken that the pins should not touch where the heart was supposed to be; but when a speedy death was desired, the pins were stuck over the region of the heart. Actual instances of the employment of the *corp chre* or *corp chreadh*, clay body or clay corpse (as Dr. Maclagan calls it), are given by the two authors last cited, one of which occurred about the year 1899. This practice is merely the continuance of old customs, for 'King James in his *Daemonology*, says that "the devil teacheth how to make pictures of wax or clay, that by roasting thereof, the persons that they bear the name of may be continually melted or dried away by continual sickness"; and in the eleventh century certain Jews, it was believed, made a waxen image of Bishop Eberhard, set about with tapers, bribed a clerk to baptize it, and set fire to it on the Sabbath, the which image burning

away at the middle, the bishop fell grievously sick and died' [70, 124].

Many magical practices and beliefs are difficult to classify as either contagious or homoeopathic magic; they may even be a mixture of both. Such is the belief in the power of names or words, talismans and amulets, divination, and various practices of public and private magic. These will be dealt with under separate headings.

II. Magical Power of Names and Words

Objection to names being mentioned of people, fairies, and animals —
names of power — satire — geis — tabu

A NAME IS considered by backward folk to be part and parcel of a living being, and as magic can be performed on a person through tangible substances that have come into contact with him, so magic can be performed or influence exerted through the utterance of a person's name. In the west of Ireland and in Torres Straits people have refused to tell me their names, though there was no objection to someone else giving me the information; the idea evidently being that by telling their own name to a stranger they were voluntarily putting themselves into the power of that stranger, who, by the knowledge of their name so imparted, could affect them in some way. Over the greater part of America was spread the belief in a personal soul, which is neither the bodily life, nor yet the mental power, but a sort of spiritual body. In many tribes, writes Dr. Brinton [7, 277], this third soul or 'astral body' bore a relation to the private personal name. Among the Mayas and Nahuas, it was conferred or came into existence with the name; and for this reason the personal name was sacred and rarely uttered. The name was thus part of the individuality, and through it the soul could be injured. Professor Rhŷs has shown [58, 566-7] from philological evidence, that Aryan-speaking peoples believed at one time not only that the name was a part of the man, but that it was that part of him which is termed the soul, the breath of life.' The dislike of hearing their names mentioned is not confined to human beings, for, as is well known, in the British Islands the Fairies have a very strong repugnance to being so called; hence they should be termed the Weefolk, the Good People, or by other ambiguous terms. Certain Scottish and English fishermen believe that the salmon and pig have a similar objection to being 'named,' but they do not mind being called respectively the 'red-fish' or the 'queer fellow.'

If power can be exerted over men by the use of their names, it is only reasonable to believe that spirits and deities can be similarly influenced. Torres Straits islanders believe that a local bogey or a spirit-girl can be summoned by being mentioned by name [29, v. 14, 86], as the witch of Endor brought up the spirit of Samuel. Dr. Frazer [20, i. 443-6] gives examples to show that people have believed that gods must keep their true names secret, lest other gods or even men should be able to conjure with them; even Ra, the great Egyptian god of the sun, declared that the name given him by his father and mother, 'remained hidden in my body since my birth, that no magician might have magic power over me.' This probably was one reason why the real name of supreme Gods was known but to a chosen few; one instance will suffice. To the Mohammedans, Allah is but an epithet in place of the Most Great Name; for, according to a Moslem belief, the secret of the latter is committed to prophets and apostles alone. Another reason is that the utterance of these secret names gives tremendous power, for [42, 273] those who know the Most Great Name of God can, by pronouncing it, transport themselves from place to place at will, can kill the living, raise the dead to life, and work other miracles.

According to Jewish tradition, when Lilith, Adam's first wife, refused to yield obedience to him she uttered the Shemhamphorash, that is, pronounced the ineffable name of Jehovah and instantly flew away. This utterance evidently gave her such power that even Jehovah could not coerce her, and the three angels, Snoi (Sennoi), Snsnoi (Sansennoi), and Smnglf (Sammangeloph), who were sent after her, were contented with a compromise, and Lilith swore by the name of the Living God that she would refrain from doing any injury to infants wherever and whenever she should find those angels, or their names, or their pictures, on parchment or paper, or on whatever else they might be drawn, 'and for this reason', says a rabbinical writer, 'we write the names of these angels on slips of paper or parchment, and bind them upon infants, that Lilith seeing them, may remember her oath; and may abstain from doing our infants any injury' [1, 165]. The custom is still maintained in the east of London of printing portions of Scripture and these three names on pieces of paper, which are placed on the four walls of a room where a baby is expected, where they remain eight days for a boy and twenty days for a girl.

Apart from the coercive power which is attributed to the pronouncing of names, there is an analogous belief in the utterance of words or phrases. Those Words of Power have been classed by Mr.

Clodd [11, 194] as:

(1) Creative Words;
(2) Mantrams and their kin;
(3) Passwords;
(4) Spells or Invocations for conjuring up the spirit of the dead, or for exorcising demons, or for removing spells on the living; and
(5) Cure-charms in formula, or magic words. Mr. Clodd points out that these classes overlap and intermingle.

Even among such backward people as the Australians, certain of the medicine-men or sorcerers were bards who devoted their poetic faculties to the purposes of enchantment, such as the Bunjil-yenjin of the Kurnai, whose peculiar branch of magic was composing and singing potent love charms and the arrangement of marriages by elopement spells [35, 356, 274].

In few countries was the spoken word more effective than in ancient Ireland; a sorcerer, whether a Druid or not, would stand on one foot, with one arm outstretched and with one eye shut, and chant an incantation in a loud voice [37, i. 240]. The grand weapon of the Irish poets by which they enforced their demands was the satire. A poet could compose a satire that would blight crops, dry up milch cows, and raise an ulcerous blister on the face. A story is told [37, i. 454] of Senchan Torpest, chief poet of Ireland, who lived in the seventh century, that once when his dinner was eaten in his absence by rats, he muttered a satire beginning, 'Rats, though sharp their snouts, are not powerful in battle', which killed ten of them on the spot. Shakespeare, and other Elizabethan writers, often refer to the belief that Irish bards could rhyme rats to death. The Irish *geis* or *geas* [pronounced gesh or gass], plural *geasa* [gassa], was the exact equivalent of an ordinary tabu, but people sometimes put an injunction on a person in some such form as 'I place you under heavy *geasa*, which no true champion will break through, to do so and so.' In this manner, the witch-lady forces Finn to search for the ring she had dropped into the lake; and Marbhan put the arch-poet Senchan Torpest under *geasa* to obtain a copy of a lost story. When the request was reasonable or just the abjured person could not refuse without loss of honour and reputation and probably in early days personal harm would accrue if the *geasa* were disregarded. The power of the *geis* was so strong that when Grania put Diarmuid under *geasa* of danger and destruction to elope with her, he was advised by his friends against his will to agree: Oisin said, 'You are not guilty if the bonds were laid on you,' and Osgar said, 'It is a pitiful man that would break his bonds' [25, 347, 8].

Sympathetic magic bulks largely in the life of backward peoples, not merely in the form of actions to be performed, but also in those to be abstained from. The 'Thou shalt not' is more in evidence than 'Thou shalt.' The prohibitions of savages and barbarians are now spoken of under the general term of tabu. Some tabus are rational from our point of view, others seem to us to be utterly irrational, but this does not affect their validity in any way. So much has been written on this subject by divers writers that only one or two examples need be given here. The subject is again referred to on p. 55.

The old Irish tale, the 'Bruiden Da Derga', tells of the destruction following the violation of tabus. Conaire, King of Ulster, was put under certain *geasa* by his father, such as: 'Thou shalt not go *desiul* round Tara nor withershins round Bregia'. 'The evil beasts of Cerna must not be hunted by thee', 'There shall not go before thee three Reds to the house of Red', and others. But on the way to Da Derga's Hostel 'They went righthandwise round Tara, and left-handwise round Bregia, and the evil beasts of Cerna were hunted by him, but he saw it not till the chase had ended.' Then he saw three red men going before him to the house of Red, and Conaire says, 'All my *geasa* have seized me tonight,' and before the next day Conaire and all his host were destroyed in Da Derga's Hostel [66, xxii.]. When Cuchulain was on his way to his last combat, he met three hags, daughters of a wizard, all blind of the left eye. They were cooking a dog with poisons and spells on spits of a rowan tree. It was *geis* to Cuchulain to eat at a cooking-hearth, or to eat the flesh of a hound, but the women put him on his honour not to refuse the piece they offered him, so he took it, and all the strength went out of the left hand in which he took the food [66, hi.].

lll. Talismans and Amulets

Stones and metals, colour, bones, teeth, claws, etc. —
lucky pig — amulets against the evil eye — luck-bone

IN THE FORMS of magic we have hitherto considered, something is done by a human being, whether by action, representation, or word, but there is another branch of magic in which the virtue resides intrinsically in certain objects which are variously termed charms, talismans, amulets, or mascots. Those that transmit qualities or are worn for good luck may be termed talismans, while the term amulet may be restricted with advantage to those charms which are preventive in their action; but the same charm is in some cases employed for both these purposes. These objects are continuously effective without any action on the part of the preparer or wearer, as they possess power in their own right, but this is from very diverse causes.

Certain stones from their colour suggest flesh; thus garnets and carnelians are worn in the rough or worked into beads as amulets against skin diseases. Most precious stones are credited with distinctive properties, and some have a reputation for being unlucky, as for example the precious opal. The amethyst, as its name implies, was regarded by the ancient Greeks as a charm against becoming intoxicated; among the ancient Egyptians the amethyst corresponded to the Zodiacal sign of the Goat, and as the goat was an enemy to vines, so the amethyst was a foe to wine. Leland [43, 351] points out that it also 'drives away bad thoughts and confers ripe and happy genius.' Amber beads are carried by people of various races for weak eyes, and it is essential they should be looked through to strengthen the sight [43, 267]. The electrical power of attraction of light objects by amber when rubbed was doubtless one cause of its supposed virtue. The several metals have their active magical properties. A lump of crude antimony in Italy is very efficacious when the following invocation is pronounced: 'Antimony, who art of zinc and copper! thou most powerful, I keep thee ever by me, that thou mayest banish from me evil people, and bring good luck to me.' Gold is the most genial or luck-bringing, and, as a woman said, 'antimony is stronger than lead, because it consists of three metals, or rather always has in it copper and lead' [43, 373-4].

Colour alone has its magical qualities, hence the frequency of red woollen thread or stuff in counter-charms against the evil eye, as an old saw expresses it: 'Roan tree and red thread, will drive the witches aa wud' [49, 156]. For the same reason red coral is so greatly valued. Blue is of equal efficacy, hence the wearing of turquoise by so many Oriental and North African peoples, and blue beads are worn by people for much the same reason, that they suspend them round the necks of donkeys or camels.

When dealing with contagious magic, we saw that many objects are worn, in order that certain qualities of the animals from which they were obtained may be imparted to the wearer. The wild boar's tusk, the acquisition of which is greatly desired by the natives of the Papuan Gulf as a mark of bravery, is coveted not so much as a personal ornament, as for the courage, ferocity, and daring which it is supposed to contain and to be capable of imparting to anyone who wears it [33, 427]. Probably this is the reason why boars' tusks are so much prized all over New Guinea, where they are wrought into 'ornaments,' which are carried in the mouth or worn on the chest when on the warpath. In West Africa the bones from the legs of tortoises are much valued as anklets, in order to give the wearers endurance. The lower jaw-bone of the tortoise is worn by certain tribes as a preventive against toothache; in this case the reason would seem to be that as the tortoise has no teeth, it cannot suffer from toothache, and thus freedom from toothache can be imparted by that edentulous jaw. The spinal bones of snakes are strung together for a girdle as a cure for backache [3, 237].

Africans, according to Arnot [3, 237], believe largely in preventive measures, and their charms are chiefly of that order. In passing through a country where leopards and lions abound, they carefully provide themselves with the claws, teeth, lips, and whiskers of those animals, and hang them around their necks, to secure themselves against being attacked. For the same purpose the point of an elephant's trunk is generally worn by the elephant-hunters. A large class of talismans consists of models or representations of objects, and the attributes of the original pass on to the symbol. The pig, perhaps on account of its abundant fecundity, was primarily sacred to the earth goddess, whether she was known as Demeter, Ceres, or by any other name. Leland points out [43, 255] that little gold and silver pigs were offered to Ceres, who was pre-eminently a goddess of fertility, and therefore of good luck and all genial influences. For these reasons they were worn by Roman ladies, and 'lucky pigs' are still very common charms, especially in South Germany.

The belief in the evil eye is not only widely spread, but extremely ancient, and in some places is still firmly rooted among the folk. 'Overlooking' may be intentional, but it is believed that many persons, without intention and even against their will, by the glance of their eye, have caused injurious effects; so that, in some cases, mothers would not venture to expose their infants to the look of their own fathers. Plutarch [18, 13] vouches for this, and admits that envy exerts an evil influence through the eyes, and adds that it is wise to employ charms and antidotes to turn aside these evil glances. A friend of his stated that some even fascinate themselves by their own gaze, and alluded to the story of Eutelidas, who, like Narcissus, fell a victim to the admiration he felt for his own likeness. Women and children seem to have been accounted by all old classical writers as the most liable to injury. Among the Greeks and Romans statues of Nemesis were erected which were adored and invoked to save their worshippers from fascination. In Rome, according to Pliny, special laws were enacted against injury to crops by incantation, excantation, or fascination [18, 15].

'Eat not the bread of him that hath an evil eye 'is just as much a maxim today as it was in the time of Solomon, and Mr. Elworthy says [18, 107] in Naples, at the appearance of a person having this reputation, a cry of 'Jettatore!' is passed, and even in a crowded street it causes an instantaneous vanishing of everybody—a rush up entries, into shops, or elsewhere. Ever since the establishment of the religious orders, monks have had the special reputation of possessing the fatal influence. The last Pope, but one, Pius the Ninth, was firmly believed to have had the evil eye. A Roman would candidly say: 'Nothing succeeds with anybody or anything when he wishes well to it.' When he went to St. Agnese to hold a great festival, down went the floor, and the people were all smashed together. Then he visited the column to the Madonna in the Piazza di Spagna, and blessed it and the workmen; of course, one fell from the scaffold the same day and killed himself [18, 23, 25].

Domestic animals always have been considered as peculiarly susceptible to this evil influence. Cows are particularly liable to fascination in Scotland, while in England of all animals the pig is most often 'overlooked.' The Turk and the Arab think the same of their horses and camels; above all the Neapolitan cabman of today believes in the great danger to his horse from the eye of the *jettatore*. The commonest of all ancient Egyptian amulets, except the scarab, was 'the Eye of Osiris,' as it is called by us. These mystic eyes were worn equally by the living and the dead as amulets; it being natural, from the associations of homœopathic magic, that representations of the eye itself should have been considered potent amulets against its malign influence. All the peoples round the Mediterranean employed representations of eyes as amulets. In Syria and Cairo necklaces composed of flat glass eyes are sold to the present day, and eye-designs protect the clothes, horse trappings, and many of the objects of daily use of the Moors [72, 211].

Plutarch declares that the objects that are fixed up to ward off witchcraft or fascination derive their efficacy from the fact that they act through the strangeness and ridiculousness of their forms, which fix the mischief-working eye upon themselves.

It was this firm belief, says Elworthy [18, 143], which led to the design of those extremely grotesque figures, of which the ancient Romans were so fond; indeed, anything that was ridiculous or indecent was supposed to be a corrective to the harmful influence of fascination. Amulets which protect against this power are of three classes:

(1) Those the object of which was to attract upon themselves the harmful glance (those were necessarily exposed to view);

(2) charms worn or carried secretly; and

(3) written words of Scripture, Koran, and other sacred writings, or cabalistic figures and formulae [18, 149].

The crescent moon was a symbol of many deities, Parvati, Devaki, and other Indian goddesses, Isis, Athena or Minerva, Artemis or Diana and the Madonna. Artemis or Diana was the patroness of domestic animals as well as of the wild creatures of the wood [21, 14];

hence Ave may trace the extreme prevalence of amulets symbolic of their attributes upon horses. The crescent—that is the horned moon—and horns appear to be interchangeable: thus horns, in one form or another, are of all objects the most common as amulets against the evil eye, whether affecting man or beast; so much so, that at last it has come to be fully believed by the Neapolitans, that in default of a horn, in coral or other form, the mere utterance of the word *corno* or *cornea* ('horn') is an effectual protection. In Italy, particularly in Naples, the cart harness is literally made up of charms and prophylactics, such as feathers, hair, brightly coloured ribbons, and especially objects of shining brass; of the last the crescent is the most common.

It would take too long to describe all the objects that are employed to counteract the evil eye in Italy alone. The following may be mentioned: fish, snakes, and various other animals, tigers' teeth, keys, a hunchback *(gobbo)*. A single pendent horn, whether of coral, shell, or metal is extremely common, as are miniature hands, these frequently have all the dibits closed up except the index and little finger, which are fully extended. This is a potent gesture, and a Neapolitan's right hand is almost constantly in that position pointing downwards, just as the hand-charms are made to hang downwards, as a prophylactic against unknown or unsuspected attacks [18, 261]. Dr. Westermarck has recently [72, 211] given an illuminating description of the use and representations of the hand against the evil eye in Morocco.

On studying various kinds of talismans and amulets, it at once becomes evident that while some are credited with contagious sympathy, others are mimetic or symbolic, that is homoeopathic in their action, while there are many others that owe their efficacy to an intimate relation with a spiritual being of some kind or other, or with a deity. The charms of this third group are to be regarded as fetishes so long as the recognition lasts that they are dependent for their virtue upon these extraneous beings; but when this belief is lost the charm becomes a mere talisman or amulet. The change from a fetish to a luck-object is constantly taking place owing to the despiritualising effect of increasing civilization. To take one example, Mr. E. Lovett first drew my attention to the 'luck bones' that are worn by Whitby, and probably by other Yorkshire, fishermen, and another friend subsequently continued the fact that these bones not only bring good fortune but are safeguards against drowning. The bone in question being the T-shaped hyoid- or tongue-bone of a sheep, Mr. Lovett suggested that this bone might have something to do with Thor's hammer. Later Professor Boyd Dawkins showed me the identical bone worn for a similar purpose by Manx fishermen, and it is worthy of note that there were Scandinavian settlements at both Whitby and the Isle of Man. I informed Herr E. Friedel of these facts and inferences, and he discovered [22, 412] that the men in the Berlin slaughter-yards have a similar custom, the end of the long arm of the bone being perforated for a thread that is fastened round the neck of the wearer. On looking into the archaeological evidence he found that in the early iron age unmistakable representations of Thor's hammer were worn as charms in Denmark and Schleswig-Holstein.

In those early days there can be little doubt that the influence of the god passed into the models of his weapon, and that these objects partook of the nature of fetishes, but later the symbols of the god degenerated into luck-objects.

IV. Divination

MEN NOT ONLY attempt to act directly upon nature, but they usually exhibit a keen desire to be guided as to the best course to take when in doubt, difficulty, or danger, and to be forewarned of the future. The practice of divination is by no means confined to professional magicians, or even to soothsayers, but any one may employ the accessory means. Any object may be used in divination: thus in Europe, as in Torres Straits [29, v. 361], a stick may be dropped to indicate a direction to be taken; or coins may be spun or dice thrown. Divination by means of skulls was common in Torres Straits [29, v. 362]; in this case the spirit of the dead person was supposed to give the required advice. Haruspication, or divination by means of certain viscera, was largely employed by the Romans, and I have several times seen a pig's liver used in Borneo for the same purpose [28, 336, 354]. In these instances the message, as indicated by the state of the particular viscus, was obtained from a deity. Other examples and varieties of divination are given by Tylor [71, i. 123].

V. Public and Private Magic

MAGIC MAY BE employed for public purposes or for private ends. In the former case it is almost invariably for the public weal, in the latter it is most frequently nefarious.

A. PUBLIC MAGIC

Australian intichiuma totem ceremonies —
corn planting dance of the Musquakie

Among some totemic peoples the men of a totem group perform magical ceremonies for the benefit of the community. The best examples of this communal magic, as it might be termed, are those described by Messrs. Baldwin Spencer and Gillen [64, 179-183] as practiced by the Arunta tribe of Central Australia at the intichiuma ceremonies. For example, the headman of a local group of the Emu totem and some other Emu men opened a vein and allowed their blood to stream on a patch of smooth ground, until about three yards were saturated. On the hard surface of the clotted blood the sacred design of the Emu totem was painted with white, yellow, red, and black. It represented certain parts of the emu; two large patches of yellow indicated lumps of fat, of which the natives are very fond, but the greater part represented, by means of circles and circular patches, the eggs in various states of development, some before and some after laying. Various sinuous lines indicated parts of the intestine. Throughout the ceremony the headman was treated with the greatest deference, and no one spoke to him except in a whisper. The sacred wooden slabs *(churinga)* were placed on one side of the painting. In the intervals of a monotonous chant the headman explained the drawing. Three men wore a headdress which represented the long neck and small head of the emu; with a curious gliding movement, they approached the spectators, occasionally stopping and moving only their heads, imitating the aimless gazing about of the bird.

The witchetty grub intichiama ceremony [64, 170-179] is performed at a special cave, where lies a large block of quartzite surrounded by small rounded stones. The former represents the perfect insect, and the latter its eggs. The headman and his associates tap the large stone and chant songs, the burden of which is an invitation to the insect to lay eggs; the headman strikes each man with one of the small stones, saying, 'You have eaten much food.' Later they go to a large rock which they tap, and invite the animal to come from all directions and lay eggs. After various symbolic ceremonies they enter a long, narrow booth made of bushes, which represents the chrysalis case from which the perfect insect emerges, and there they sing of the animal in its various stages and of the sacred stones.

There are many similar ceremonies which the men of a totem

group make in order to increase or produce their particular totem; thus, taking the tribe as a whole, the object of these ceremonies is that of increasing the total food supply (64, 315-319). Among the Arunta and Ilpirra only the men of the totem are allowed to be present or to take part in the actual ceremony. During its progress there is always some ceremony, such as that of allowing the blood of young men of the totem to flow over the stone which is associated with the ancestors of the totem. The idea of this is to send the spirits of the animals out of the stone to replenish the stock of the totemic animal. After the ceremony, when, as a consequence, the animal or plant has become abundant, the men of all classes and totems go out and bring supplies into the main camp. No one as yet may eat it. The headman of the totem, in the presence of all in camp, solemnly eats a little and hands the remainder over to the men of the other totems, telling them to eat freely. If the headman did not eat a little he would lose the power of performing intichiuma successfully.

In other tribes to the north similar ceremonies exist, but they are less elaborate and sometimes of the simplest description. The headman of the white cockatoo totem group and his son spent the whole of one night 'singing' the cockatoo. In the Wara tribe on the shore of the Gulf of Carpentaria a man of the rain-group goes to a pool, and, taking care that no women or strangers are in sight, bends down over and 'sings' the water; then he takes some up in his hands, drinks it, and spits it out in various directions. After that, he throws water all over himself, and after scattering some all round, he returns quietly to his camp, and the rain is supposed to follow

(64, 314). There is very little difference between this act and ordinary individual magic, the essential distinction being that the man in this case makes rain by virtue of rain being his totem, it is a function of human male members of the totem group to increase their totem.

When the totemic system falls into decay, there seems to be a tendency for the old magical ceremonies which had for their purport the increase of the totem, to be performed by certain families, rather than by groups of men; this appears to be associated with the growth of property in land, so that in time the performance of certain ceremonies is restricted to a single man, who transmits the right to his son, and they alone of the community have this duty. There is nothing to distinguish men with these rights from ordinary sorcerers who practice definite departments of magic.

A very large number of examples of public magical ceremonies, undertaken for the good of the community, have been collected by Dr. Frazer in his *Golden Bough*; of especial interest are those connected with the production of abundant harvests, and the active participation of women in such customs is very significant. I here give an example, recently published by Miss Mary Owen (56, 60). The Corn-planting dance of the Musquakie or Fox Indians, takes place in April, though the real corn-planting commences about the 1st of May. It is danced by men only; they trot at sunrise along the east side of a cornfield selected by the shaman, going in single file with their rattles and little tambourines or prayer drums, while a young maiden goes into the field and plants a few grains from a perfect ear handed to her by the Honourable Women (women who have borne sons). If the harvest of the year before was scant the dancers may go entirely round the field. Afterwards there is some eating and drinking, but not an elaborate feast. Formerly the real planting of the field followed the ceremonial, and no food was eaten until the women had finished planting. Another old custom was to have the maid who did the planting given a husband, who went with her into the field. Later a prophet had a revelation that this custom should cease. The day is at the present time a favourite one for weddings.

B. PRIVATE MAGIC

Folk-remedies — love-charms — nefarious magic

Individuals frequently practice magic for private ends, of which the objects to be attained may be perfectly legitimate or even praise-worthy, but more frequently recourse is had to magical practices for harmful purposes. Folk remedies for sickness and pains are very frequently of a purely magical character. For example, a common cure for warts is to rub them with a piece of raw meat, which must then be buried; as the meat decays so will the warts disappear: to be effective the meat should be stolen. A woman in Islay was cured of toothache by a man driving a nail into the upper lintel of the kitchen door; he told her to keep it there, and, should it become loose at any time, to tap it a little with a hammer until it had a grip, and he assured her she would be free from toothache. She never again suffered from toothache [49, 158]. Any variety or combination of varieties of sympathetic magic may be employed in the manufacture or practice of love-charms; frequently they are fortified by the subtle association of scent. Doubtless certain scents have a direct stimulating effect, but, apart from this, should any scent be definitely worn when young men wish to attract girls, there can be no doubt that the suggestion would tend to act powerfully upon the latter, and that 'girl-medicine,' as l have heard it called, would of itself be potent even if other practices were not employed. l was told by a Torres Straits islander that just as a snake that is in one tree can, by swallowing its spittle, make a bird that is in another tree come to it, so if a man chews a certain medicine and a girl sees him swallowing the infusion in his saliva, she understands what the man means and is constrained to go to him [29, v. 328]. Various instances of nefarious magic have been given in the preceding pages. A good example came under my own observation. In Torres Straits there is a vine-like plant that loses its leaves at a certain season of the year, and the stem breaks up into joints, which often bear a striking resemblance to some of the long bones of the human skeleton. This circumstance led magicians to employ these sticks to make human beings into similar dried and shrivelled-up objects. The dry segments of the vine were collected and the magician gave the name of some part of the body to each joint: for example, one would be called an 'arm,' another a 'leg' and so forth. The magician crouched like a fish-eagle and, imitating the way that a bird tears flesh off bones, threw the segments behind him without looking round. If he left the spot without turning round to look at the sticks the patient would die; but if he did not wish to proceed to this extremity, he turned and looked at the segments, and subsequently he would return and pick them up and place them together and put 'medicine' on them, and the patient would recover [29, v. 325].

The following account recently published by Mrs. J. Gunn [26, 98] is so characteristic that I quote it nearly verbatim. In Northern Australia anyone can 'sing magic' even lubras [women], but of course the wise old magic men do it best. It never fails with them, particularly if they 'sing' and point one of the special 'death-bones' or 'sacred stones' of the tribe. Generally a black fellow goes away quite by himself when he is 'singing magic,' but very occasionally a few men join together, as they did in the case of 'Goggle Eye'. When enough magic has been 'sung' into the bone, it is taken away to the camp, and very secretly pointed at the unconscious victim. The magic spirit of the bone runs into the man who is pointed at, and gradually kills him. Of course the man who has been 'sung' must be told somehow, or he will not get a fright and die. There are many ways of managing this; one very good way is to put the bone where he will be sure to find it, in his dilly-bag, or near his fire, or through the handle of his spear; but the man who leaves the bone about must, of course, be very careful to destroy his own tracks. 'Goggle Eye', after he had found the bones lying about, knew exactly what was going to happen to him, and of course it did. His throat got very sore, and he grew so thin and weak that he could hardly stand. A man can be cured by magic men charming the 'bone' away again; but 'Goggle Eye' was old, and, what was worse, he was getting very cross, and too fond of ordering people about, so the black fellows thought it would be the best plan not to cure him, and a few more sneaked away into the bush and 'sang' some more bones, and pointed them at him to make quite sure about his dying. Poor old 'Goggle Eye' suffered dreadfully; no native would help him except his blood brother, because they were afraid of the curse coming to them. Some said they would like to help, but that if they made 'Goggle Eye's' fire for him, their own would never burn again. Nobody could even carry his food to him. Soon after, at 'fowl sing out,' or cockcrow, he died.

VI. Magicians

Training of sorcerers and societies of magicians

MOST FORMS OF magic can be performed by anybody provided he knows what to do; but there are specialists in magic, who, by us, are variously termed medicine-men, magicians, sorcerers, wizards, witches, wise women, and the like. Their lore is transmitted orally to their disciples, who may or may not be their own children. Magical powers may be due to the mere accident of birth, as for example in the European belief in the therapeutic gifts of the seventh son of a seventh son. In some cases the sorcerer has to undergo a rigorous training, often being subjected to painful or loathsome ordeals; by these means the weaklings are eliminated, and those who persist have their character and fortitude strengthened, and they gain increased respect from their fellowmen. Further, in Australia and elsewhere, the medicine man is not always a 'doctor'; he may be a 'rainmaker', 'seer', or 'spirit-medium', or may practice some special form of magic.

Usually the sorcerers unite together to form a society, which may attain great influence among backward races. According to

Leland [43, 10], 1 there is actually in Tuscany a culture or worship of fetishes which are not Catholic, i.e. of strange stones and many curious relics. But there is a great deal of mystery and secrecy observed in all this cult. It has its professors; men, but mostly women, who collect charms and spells, and teach them to one another, and hold meetings; that is, there is a kind of college of witches and wizards, which, for many good reasons, eludes observation.' The old faith, as it is termed, is pre-Christian, but not actively anti-Christian.

VII. The Psychology of Magical Practices

Nervous instability — suggestion — make-believe — tabu — mana —
projective will-power or telepathy — from spell to prayer —
the impossible not undertaken — loopholes in case of failure

THE SUPERFICIAL OBSERVER is apt to regard the medicine-men or sorcerers as cheats who deliberately humbug their neighbours; but it is probable that most of them really believe themselves to be possessed of occult or supernormal power. Doubtless they do many things for mere effect, in order to enhance the respect they desire to have paid to themselves personally, as well as to put the subjects or spectators into a proper frame of mind; but this is precisely what is deliberately done by the organizers of all ceremonies by all peoples. Doubtless, also, many acts are performed which are intended to impose upon the credulity of others; but this is a device which is not unknown among cultured people, as, for example, the liquefying of the blood of St. Januarius in Naples. There remain, however, a large number of phenomena, which are as mysterious to them as they are to the vast majority of mankind, and many of these are receiving the attention of psychologists of the present day, without their significance being understood. Mr. Podmore [55, 373] is not afraid to say that 'many of the alleged wonders of witchcraft and of ancient magic in general, when disentangled from the accretions formed round them by popular myth and superstition, present a marked resemblance to some of the facts recorded' in his book.

The mental equilibrium of many backward peoples is very unstable, although they may not suffer from the same derangements of the nervous system that affect the more highly civilized peoples. To take an example or two of this nervous instability, Castren observed long ago that if the Samoyeds were sitting around inside their skin tents in the evening, and someone crept up and struck the tent, half of them were likely to fall into cataleptic fits. Bogoras [5, 42] refers to the well-known Arctic hysteria which is so widespread among the Yukaghir and Lamut women, and to a less extent among the Chukchee, the Russianised, and even the Russian women. This disease develops chiefly in the form of an uncontrollable desire to repeat in a loud voice each word spoken by somebody else, and to imitate every sudden gesture or action. This is the same nervous disorder as the widely spread la toh of Malaysia, which has been so admirably described by Sir F. A. Swettenham [68, 64].

The far-reaching power of suggestion has been perhaps the most potent factor in upholding magical practices, especially when it is combined with hypnotism. The hypnotic state, it must be remembered, though ordinarily produced by another, can be self-induced by gazing at an object. There is an overwhelming number of modern instances of bad habits, various diseases, inflammations, local and general pain, insomnia, neurasthenia, psychic paralysis, and psychic hysteria, being cured by suggestion while the patient is in the hypnotic state [31, 607]. Conversely, pain, inflammations, and other organic changes can be produced through the same means; such is the explanation of the appearance of stigmata on the hands and feet of religious ecstatics, who had induced auto-hypnotism by intently gazing on the Figure on the Cross. The cataleptic and anaesthetic conditions producible by hypnotism are well known all over the world, and have for ages been part of the stock-in-trade of sorcerers, medicine men, or of certain religious enthusiasts.

Suggestion alone, without the aid of hypnotism, can effect wonders, and faith -cures and Christian science are by no means a new thing under the sun, but something very old under new names. Probably every physician has known cases of 'persons who died because they did not want to live or were at least indifferent: and probably an equal number who materially lengthened their lives by the mere determination not to die' [67, 612].

'The psychology of the matter, writes Marett [51, 143], 'is up to a certain point simple enough. Just as the savage is a good actor, throwing himself like a child into his mime, so he is a good spectator, entering into the spirit of another's acting, herein again resembling the child, who can be frightened into fits by the roar of what he knows to be but a "pretended" lion. Even if the make-believe is more or less make-believe to the victim, it is hardly less efficacious; for, dominating, as it tends to do, the field of attention, it racks the emotional system, and, taking advantage of the relative abeyance of intelligent thought and will, sets stirring all manner of deep lying impulses and automatisms.'

All peoples have prohibitions of certain kinds, and most have a firm belief that should these tabus be broken dire consequences will befall the offender. Occasionally the punishment is effected by the social executive, through representatives of secret societies or by other means; but usually it is left in the hands, so to speak, of the outraged spiritual powers, and so strong is this belief that it drees its own weird. For example, Father Merolla [54, xvi. 238] tells of a young Congo negro who, being on a journey, lodged at a friend's house; the latter got a wild hen for his breakfast, and the young man asked if it were a wild hen. His host replied 'No.' Then he fell on heartily, and afterwards proceeded on his journey. After four years these two met together again, and his old friend asked him 'If he would eat a wild hen, to which he answered that it was tabooed to him.' Hereat the host began immediately to laugh, inquiring of him, "What made him refuse it now, when he had eaten one at his table about four years ago?" At the hearing of this the negro immediately fell a-trembling, and suffered himself to be so far possessed with the effects of imagination that he died in less than twenty-four hours after.' Armit [2, 459] relates that an Australian died of fright within a fortnight after he had discovered his sick wife had lain upon his blanket. Nowhere is the power of taboo greater than among the Polynesians. And examples of its potency in procuring its own fulfilment in the Heroic Age of Ireland have already been given.

No wonder then that belief in the magical powers of sorcerers can cause the same effects. Messrs. Spencer and Gillen [64, 537] state that the Australian natives believe that any bone, stick, spear, etc., which has been 'sung' is supposed to be endowed with what the natives call *Arungquiltha*, that is, magical poisonous properties, and any native who believes that he has been struck by, say, a charmed spear, is almost sure to die, whether the wound be slight or severe, unless he be saved by the counter magic of a medicine-man. He simply lies down, refuses food, and pines away. Actual instances are given of men with slight wounds, dying in a few days from this belief.

There can be no doubt that magical practices can act by suggestion through fear and fascination upon human victims who are aware of their occurrence, and it is probable that in most cases the victim is made aware of such practices as in the instance given on p. 49. Also there is every reason to believe that all backward peoples, including the sorcerers themselves, believe in the power of magic. Casalis [10, 275] gives an instructive instance in point. A chief of the Basutos once held forth in his presence on the matter of sorcery: he said, Sorcery only exists in the mouths of those who speak of it. It is no more in the power of man to kill his fellow by the mere effect of his will, than it would be to raise him from the dead. This is my opinion. Nevertheless, you sorcerers who hear me speak, use moderation.'

Probably more widely spread than is usually accepted is the belief of some backward peoples, and therefore of their magicians, in a spiritual force that accomplishes their desires; such, for example, as the mana of the Melanesians. 'The Melanesian mind,' writes Dr. Codrington [12, 118], 'is entirely possessed by the belief in a supernatural power or influence, called almost universally *mana*. This is what works to effect everything which is beyond the ordinary power of man, outside the common processes of nature; it is present in the atmosphere of life, attaches itself to persons and to things, and is manifested by results which can only be ascribed to its operation. When one has got it he can use it and direct it, but its force may break forth at some new point; the presence of it is ascertained by proof. A man comes by chance upon a stone which takes his fancy; its shape is singular, it is like something, it is certainly not a common stone, there must be *mana* in it. So he argues with himself, and he puts it to the proof; he lays it at the root of a tree to the fruit of which it has a certain resemblance, or he buries it in the ground when he plants a garden; an abundant crop on the tree or in the garden shows that he is right, the stone is *mana*, has that power in it. Having that power, it is a vehicle to convey *mana* to other stones. In the same way certain forms of words, generally in the form of a song, have power for certain purposes; a charm of words is called *mana*. But this power, though itself impersonal, is always connected with some person who directs it; all spirits have it, ghosts generally, some men. If a stone is found to have a supernatural power it is because a spirit has associated itself with it. A dead man's bone has with it *mana*, because the ghost is with the bone; a man may have so close a connection with a spirit or ghost that he has *mana* in himself also, and can so direct it as to effect what he desires. All conspicuous success is a proof that a man has *mana*; his influence depends on the impression made on the people's mind that he has it.' If a man has been successful in fighting, it is not through his own qualities, but 'he has certainly got the *mana*of some deceased warrior to empower him, conveyed in an amulet of a stone round his neck, or a tuft of leaves in his belt, in a tooth hung upon the finger of his bow hand, or in the form of words with which he brings supernatural assistance to his side.' The Omaha [19] believe that a man's own will can act directly on his fellows by singing certain songs; this act is called *wazhin-dhedhe*, that is 'directive energy, to send'; the Omaha term 'signifies to send forth one's thought and will power toward another in order to supplement his strength, and thereby affect his action,' or, as we should term it, telepathy. By an appeal to Wakanda (that is 'immanent life manifest in all things, or the hidden and mysterious power which brings to pass'), in the rite of vision, the man's powers could be supplemented by the co-operation of the elements and of animals.

The innate spirituality of the savage appears to be largely ignored by students, who usually dub the magic worker as a conscious cheat and humbug, whereas it seems to be more correct to regard him as dealing with material objects, mainly as endowed with life [Animism; 50, 171], or as the vehicles of spiritual or supernatural power, and by means of such objects or by the shafts of speech he can effectively project his will.

If then, as Mr. Marett points out [51, 150], the occult projectiveness of the magical act is naturally and almost inevitably interpreted as an exertion of will that somehow finds its way to another will and dominates it, the spell or uttered 'must' will tend to embody the very life and soul of the affair. Nothing finds its way home to another's mind more sharply. It is the very type of a spiritual projectile.

In many examples of magical procedure the magician appears to act directly upon nature, and seeks to enforce the action of his will by the power of the spoken word or spell. In other cases he obtains power from energy derived from something outside of himself; for example, the shaman of Siberia may be possessed by a spirit, or the magician may even be possessed by a god. Thus, by insensible stages do we arrive at actions that may better be described as religious or theurgic than as magical. Numerous examples of transition stages are given by Mr. W. W. Skeat [63]. The god-inspired magician may become an actual deity, for many royal magicians, who are more especially rain-makers, are regarded, as Dr. Frazer has recently pointed out, as incarnate gods in Africa and elsewhere [21]. Concurrently with ideas of personification and progressive deification the spell evolves into prayer. On the other hand, power may be obtained over deities by practices that are essentially magical, as, for example, by uttering the ineffable name, or by spells and incantations, and these may at the same time be associated with prayer, or the prayer itself may degenerate into a spell.

However, it may be with human beings, few culture-folk will admit that sorcerers can effect the ordinary phenomena of nature, and in this respect, at all events, they should soon become discredited. On one occasion in Murray Island, Torres Straits, a native showed me two stones in a recess on the foreshore which were pointed at by men holding certain leaves which were left there. A 'big wind' would immediately arise which lasted until the plants were removed. This zogo was employed only in the season of the South-east trade wind.

On my asking whether the ceremony was done in the Northwest monsoon, my informant said emphatically, 'Can't do it in North-west.' That is, the charm is performed only at that season of the year when the required result is possible—indeed, when it is of normal occurrence [28, 60; 29, vi.] In this, as in other cases, I found that the impossible was never attempted. A rain charm would not be made when there was no expectation of rain coming, or a southeast wind be raised during the wrong season. Probably this is the experience of others elsewhere, and thus it is not remarkable if the desired result frequently follows the performance of the charming.

A loophole is generally provided in case of failure. Either some irregularity or mistake occurred in the performance of the charm, or another sorcerer was performing contrary magic which proved of greater potency.

FETISHISM

I. Definition

1. Etymological — 2. Historical — 3. Dogmatic

THE WORD FETISHISM has been so misused of late that ethnolo-
gists are apt to view it askance and hesitate to employ it in religious
classifications. It has been stretched to such an extent in various
directions that it has lost the definition and precision necessary
for a scientific term. Starting from a humble origin, referring in its
native land (Portugal) to the charms and amulets worn 'for luck,' and
to relics of saints, 'fetish' grew to such amazing proportions when
transplanted to West African soil, that at last there was nothing
connected with West African religion to which it was not applied.
De Brosses introduced Fetichisme as a general descriptive term [8],
supposing the word to be connected with *chose fée, fatum*. Comte
employed it to describe the universal religious tendency to which
Dr. Tylor has *Philosophic Positive* given the name of Animism [71,
chaps, xi.-xvii.]. Bastholm claimed 'everything produced by nature or art,
which receives divine honour, including the sun, moon, earth, air,
fire, water, with rivers, trees, stones, images and animals, considered
as objects of divine worship, as Fetishism; and Lippert [46] defines
Fetishism as 'a belief in the souls of the departed coming to dwell in

anything that is tangible or visible in heaven or earth.'

Although Miss Kingsley [39, 139] expresses regret that the word Fetish 'is getting very loosely used in England,' she scarcely helps forward the work of distinction and arrangement when a few lines further on she announces 'When I say Fetish, or Ju Ju, I mean the religion of the natives of West Africa'. Subsequently she overstepped her own definition, describing the secret societies as 'pure fetish' [41, 139], although they 'are not essentially religious,' but 'are mainly judicial.'

The Rev. R. H. Nassau perpetuates this vague use of the word, grouping under the name of Fetishism all native customs even remotely connected, as everything is in West Africa, with religious or magical beliefs, until the ejaculation uttered when one sneezes or stumbles receives the sounding title, 'fetish prayer' [53, 97].

These 'lumpings' are all the more to be regretted since Miss Kingsley and the Rev. R. H. Nassau are among the chief authorities on West African Fetishism in its most characteristic forms, and a clear definition of the use of the word, with a rigid adherence to its proper meaning, would have done great service in preventing many misconceptions.

The meaning of any word depends upon its definition, and it may be defined in three ways:

1. etymologically;
2. historically;
3. dogmatically.

1. The word fetish is derived through the Portuguese *feiti-go* from the Latin *facticius— facere* — to do. This shows the original conception at the root of the word.

2. The historical definition shows the growth or evolution of the meaning of the word, starting from its original conception. Dr. Tylor has pointed out how magic has appropriated to itself the derivatives of 'to do' such as *feitigo* in Portuguese, *fattura* in Italian, *faiture* in Old French, and many more, thus claiming to be 'doing' *par excellence* (70, 135). This tendency is already noticeable even in classical times (*'potens et factiosus,'* possessed of power and influence, Auct. Her. 2, 26, 40), and is well marked in Plautus [1], who uses various derivatives of facere to mean 'powerful' or 'influential', especially with reference to influence due to family connection or to riches (*factiones*, Aul. n. i. 45; factiosus, ib. ll. ii. 50; *factio, Cist.* n. i. 17, etc.). From this sense of potent politically, later Latin developed the meaning of potent magically, as seen in *facturari*, to bewitch, *factura*, witchcraft, from which latter is descended the Old French faiture, witchcraft, and perhaps our slang word 'fake'. Fetish as derived from the passive form *facticius*, meaning made by art, artificial, was probably first applied to images, idols or amulets made

---

1   For the references to the suggestive use of the word by Plautus, I am indebted to Miss Rachel White of Newnham College.

by hand, and later included all objects possessing magical potency, i.e. bewitched or 'faked'.

3. The dogmatic definition of a word is the meaning attached to it by individuals of authority.

Fetishism is defined as 'the worship of inanimate objects,' the worship of stocks and stones, 'the religious worship of material objects' [61, 61], tangible and inanimate objects worshipped for themselves alone' [15, 196], and a fetish is defined as 'differing from an idol in that it is worshipped in its own character, not as the symbol, image, or occasional residence of a deity (*New English Dictionary*, Oxford, Clarendon Press, 1901).

The account of the native of Fida given by Bosman [54, xvi. 493] is often quoted as the classic example of fetishism:

I once asked a negro with whom I could talk very freely... how they celebrated their divine worship, and what number of gods they had; he, laughing, answered that I had puzzled him; and assured me that nobody in the whole country could give me an exact account of it. For, as for my own part, I have a very large number of gods, and doubt not but that others have as many. For any of us being resolved to undertake anything of importance, we first of all search out a god to prosper our designed undertaking; and going out of doors with the design, take the first creature that presents itself to our eyes, whether dog, cat, or the most contemptible creature in the world for our god: or perhaps instead of that, any inanimate that falls in our way, whether a stone, a piece of wood, or anything else of the same nature. This new-chosen god is immediately presented with an offering, which is accompanied by a solemn vow, that if it pleaseth him to prosper our undertakings, for the future we will always worship and esteem him as a god. If our design prove successful, we have discovered a new and assisting god, which is daily presented with a fresh offering j but if the contrary happen, the new god is rejected as a useless tool, and consequently returns to his primitive estate. We make and break our gods daily, and consequently are the masters and inventors of what we sacrifice to.

Bosnian goes on to say:

I was very well pleased to hear the negro talk in this manner concerning his country gods; but, having conversed with him for some time, I observed that he ridiculed his own country gods, for, having lived amongst the French, whose language he perfectly understood and spoke, he had amongst them imbibed the principles of the Christian religion, and somewhat towards a just notion of the true God and how he is to be worshipped, ... wherefore he no further concerned himself with the gods of the country than as engaged to it for quietness' sake, or to make his friends easy.

A sceptic is scarcely likely to give a sympathetic report of a religion he has discarded, and Bosnian's negro is no exception to the rule. He describes the outward, tangible aspect of fetishism, but ignores its spiritual interpretation, and the dogmatic definitions above follow in the same path of error.

Fetishism and the fetish, as thus defined, do not exist, except in 'incomplete observations'; they certainly are nowhere to be found in West Africa, the typical land of fetishism.

'Every native with whom I have conversed on the subject,' writes Ellis, 'has laughed at the possibility of it being supposed that he could worship or offer sacrifice to some such object as a stone, which of itself, it would be perfectly obvious to his senses was a stone only and nothing more' [15, 192]. So the Maori *wakapakoko* were only thought to possess virtue or peculiar sanctity from the presence of the god they represented when dressed up for worship; at other times they were regarded only as bits of ordinary wood [69, 212], and Brinton affirms that 'nowhere in the world did man ever worship a stick or a stone as such' [6, 131].

All cases of Fetishism, when examined, show that the worship is paid to an intangible power or spirit incorporated in some visible form, and that the fetish is merely the link between the worshipper and the object of his worship. Any definition, therefore which takes no account of the spiritual force behind the material object is seen to be incomplete and superficial, as it ignores the essential conception of the worship.

Dr. Tylor enlarges the scope of the word, classing Fetishism as a subordinate department of Animism, and defining it as the doctrine of spirits embodied in, or conveying influence through, certain material objects. He includes in it the worship of stocks and stones, 'and thence it passes by an imperceptible gradation into idolatry' [71, ii. 144].

It is these imperceptible gradations, which blur all the outlines of the rigid systematist, and make an exclusive classification impossible. Encouragement is found in the reflection that exclusive classifications are almost unknown to science, and, where met with, are generally due to ignorance, waiting for greater knowledge or further research to provide the intermediate links which everywhere blend class with class, species with species. But when the group is studied in its area of characterization, certain features stand prominently forward, and by a study of these the essential characteristics of the whole class can be determined.

II. Essential Characters of Fetishism

May be any object, a symbolic charm with sympathetic properties, a sign or token representing an ideal notion or being, habitation of a spiritual being, vehicle for communication of a spirit, instrument by which spirit acts — possesses personality and will — may act by own will or by foreign spirit — spirit and material object can be dissociated, worshipped, sacrificed to, talked with, petted and ill-treated

THE CHARACTERISTIC FEATURES of fetishism, and particularly of West African fetishism, are as follows:

The fetish may consist of any object whatsoever, but the object chosen is generally either a wonderful ornament or curiosity, a symbolic charm with sympathetic properties, or a sign or token representing an ideal notion or being. It is credited with mysterious power, owing to its being, temporarily or permanently, the vessel or habitation, vehicle for communication, or instrument of some unseen power or spirit, which is conceived to possess personality and will, and ability to see, hear, understand, and act. It may act by the will or force of its own power or spirit, or by force of a foreign power entering it or acting on it from without, and the material object and the power or spirit may be dissociated. It is worshipped, prayed to, sacrificed to, talked with, and petted or ill-treated with regard to its past or future behaviour. In its most characteristic form a fetish must be consecrated by a priest.

1. A fetish may be any object whatsoever, but there is always a reason for its choice. The simplest reason is that it attracts attention [61, 61] [71, ii. 145], and anything that attracts attention at once acquires an exaggerated value, and appeals to that natural instinct of human nature, found also among some birds and animals, the love for collecting.

'In the love of abnormal curiosities there shows itself a craving for the marvellous, an endeavour to get free from the tedious sense of law and uniformity in nature' [71, ii. 145].

So the fetish consists of a queer-shaped stone, a bright bead, a stick, parrots' feathers, a root, claw, seed, bone, or any curious or conspicuous object.

In Benin they take everything which seems extraordinary in nature for a god, and make offerings to him, and each is his own priest, in order to worship his gods in what manner pleases him best [54, xvi. 530].

Or the object may have attracted attention by its behaviour. A visitor to a fetish hut took up a stone about as big as a hen's egg, and its owner told its history. 'He was once going out on important business, but crossing the threshold he trod on this stone and hurt himself. Ha, ha! thought he, art thou here? So he took the stone, and it helped him through his undertaking for days' [71, ii. 158]. Sometimes the object to be chosen is revealed to a man in a dream, as among the natives of the Gold Coast, where a dead relation will return to direct a man to go to a certain spot and there select a certain stone, or piece of a tree, which he is to bring home with him, and guard and reverence as the habitation of a protecting deity [15, 90].

This connects the fetish with the guardian spirits of the North American Indians, which appear to young men in dreams, or visions, after prayer and fasting. The vision generally takes the form of some tangible object, often an animal, a portion of which is preserved by the man as his most precious possession, and if not, some concrete form is taken to represent the subject of the vision. A guardian spirit differs, however, from a fetish, in that it is a lifelong possession, some men are not privileged to obtain one, and no man could possess more than one; while any man could obtain a fetish, and could discard one and adopt another if it proved to be unavailing.

2. It consists of a symbolic charm with sympathetic properties. 'There is a relation between the selected substances and the object to be obtained: to give the possessor bravery or strength, some part of a leopard or an elephant; to give cunning, some part of a gazelle; to give wisdom, some part of a human brain; to give courage, some part of a heart; to give influence, some part of an eye, etc. etc. 'These substances are supposed to lure some spirit (being in some way pleasing to it) which thenceforward is satisfied to reside in them and to aid the possessor in the accomplishment of some specific wish' [53, 82].

For convenience of carriage these substances are put into snail-shells, nutshells, or the small horns of gazelles, or of goats, and the whole then forms the fetish.

Bosnian describes the way in which a fetish, consisting of a pipe filled with various substances, was generally made on the Guinea Coast in 1705. 'They have a great wooden pipe filled with earth, oil, blood, bones of dead men and beasts, feathers, hair, and to be short, all sorts of excrementitiously and filthy trash, which they do not endeavour to mould into any shape, but lay it in a confused heap in the pipe' [54, xvi. 398].

'Human eyeballs, particularly of white men, are a great charm. This, I fancy, is to secure the man "that lives in your eyes" for the service of the village' [40, 305].

Sometimes there is a tangible connection between the object chosen for the fetish and the spirit occupying it. Thus, among the Gold Coast natives the object which is entered by the subordinate spirit of Sasabonsum must be taken from the habitat of a Sasabonsum, from a place, that is, which is marked with red earth, where the red earth marks the blood of the victim of a Sasabonsum [15, 109].

3. It may consist of a sign or token representing an ideal notion or being, and here it is difficult to draw any distinction between fetishism and idolatry, 'for a small line and a few streaks of colour may change a fetish into an idol' [61, 77]. Certainly the lower forms of idolatry present the aspect of fetishism, but the true fetish is not shaped to resemble the spirit it represents, and the true idol is only the symbol, not the vessel, vehicle, or instrument of deity. At the same time, an image may be worshipped as a fetish, and regarded as a material body provided for a spirit; or a fetish, being regarded merely as the symbol or representative of a spirit, seems to develop the earliest form of idolatry [71, ii. 169]. The distinction lies in the attitude of mind in which the objects are worshipped, and no objective differentiation is possible, for the object will be a fetish for one worshipper and a

pure symbol of a spirit to another.

Stone worship is often pure fetishism, the stone being regarded as the tangible sign or token of a spirit or power to which worship is addressed. But it advances beyond the limits of fetishism if a general spirit, or a god of a community, while worshipped in the form of a stone, is also believed to animate other objects. The animating force of a fetish must be individual, and cannot animate more than one object at a time. When the spirits of the suhman charms [15, 99] are considered to be individual spirits dependent upon Sasabonsum they are fetishes; if the spirit of Sasabonsum were supposed to animate all the suhman charms they could not properly be called fetishes.

4. A fetish is credited with mysterious powers owing to its being the habitation, temporary or permanent, of a spiritual being. This sounds like a definition of the principle of animism, and so it may be, for fetishism is animism, seen, as it were, from the other end and seen in detail. Animism sees all things animated by spirits; fetishism sees a spirit incorporated in an individual object.

But there is this distinction, that the spirit which is believed to occupy the fetish is a different conception of the spirit of the animistic theory; it is not the soul or vital power belonging to the object, and inherent in it, from which the virtue is derived, but a spirit or power attracted to and incorporated in it, while separable from it. The spirit of the fetish is also distinct from a god, as it can animate one object only, while a god can manifest his power in various forms.

Thus, in Bosman's account of the Benin fetish quoted above, he talks of 'the pipe where the idol is lodged,' that is the material habitation into which the spirit has been lured by some means of attraction. Miss Kingsley, describing a fetish or *juju*, says 'it is not a doll or toy, and has far more affinity to the image of a saint, inasmuch as it is not venerated for itself, or treasured because of its prettiness, but only because it is the residence, or the occasional haunt, of a spirit' [40, 287].

The material objects which form the tutelary deities or *Bohsum* of the natives of the Gold Coast are not symbols of gods which usually reside elsewhere; each is the actual receptacle or ordinary abiding-place of an indwelling god. One may be a wooden figure, another a stone, a third a covered calabash or an earthen pot, containing a mixture of blood and earth [15, 80]. The best example of this class is provided by the *suhman*.

The man who wants a *suhman* takes some objects, it may be a rudely cut wooden image, or a stone, a root of a plant, or some red earth placed in a pan, and then he calls on a spirit of Sasabonsum ('a genus of deities, every member of which possesses identical characteristics') to enter the object prepared, promising it offerings and worship. If a spirit consents to take up its residence in the object a low hissing sound is heard, and the *suhman* is complete. It receives a small portion of the daily food of its owner, and is treated with reverence, and mainly used to bring evil on someone else [15, 100- 101].

5. Sometimes the fetish is merely the vehicle or means by which the spirit communicates with his worshippers, and only acquires a temporary personality when thus inspired. This is the character of the New Zealand fetishes, *wakapakoko*, or images.

'A small image was used about 18 inches long, resembling a peg, with a carved head. The priest first bandaged a fillet of red parrot feathers under the god's chin, which was called his *pahau* or beard; when this was done it was taken possession of by the *atua*, whose spirit entered it; the priest then either held it in the hand and vibrated it in the air, whilst the powerful *karakia* (charm, prayer) was repeated, or he tied a piece of string, formed of the centre of a flax leaf, round the neck of the image and stuck it in the ground: he sat at a little distance from it, holding the string in his hand, and gave the god a jerk to arrest his attention' [69, 182]. These Maori fetishes 'were only thought to possess virtue or peculiar sanctity from the presence of the god they represent when dressed up, at other times they were regarded as bits of ordinary wood' [69, 212]. The use of the words 'image' and 'god' seem to place this ceremony on a higher plane than fetishism, but the 'god' is generally the spirit of an ancestor, and the 'image' is less a portrait of a worshipped deity than an expression of the Maori genius for woodcarving.

6. While the conception of the fetish as the vehicle of communication between spirit and worshipper raises fetishism to a higher plane in religious evolution, the conception of the fetish as an instrument by which the spirit acts lowers it to a stage which is not necessarily religious at all, to a stage where the fetish is often regarded merely in the light of a charm or an amulet.

This is the lowest and the commonest form of fetishism; it may practically be said to be universal.

Bosnian relates that the word Fetiche is chiefly used in a religious sense, or at least is derived from thence, but 'all things made in honour of these false gods, never so mean, are called Fetiche.'

These material charms are so common that by the universality of their use, and the prominence given to them everywhere, in houses and on the person, they almost monopolise the religious thought of the Bantu negro, subordinating other acknowledged points of his theology, dominating his almost entire religious interest, and giving the departmental word 'fetich' such overwhelming regard that it has furnished the name distinctive of the native African religious system [53, 80]. 'The new-born infant, has a health -knot tied about his neck, wrists, or loins, and down to the day of oldest age everyone keeps on multiplying or renewing or altering these life talismans' [53, 85].

It is interesting to find this form of fetish charm described by Bosnian at the beginning of the eighteenth century.

'The child is no sooner born than the priest (here called Fetichee or Confoe) is sent for, who binds a parcel of ropes and coral and other trash about the head, body, arms, and legs of the infant; after which he exorcises, according to their accustomed manner, by which they believe it is armed against all sickness and ill accidents, and doubtless this is as effectual as if done by the Pope himself [54, xvi. 388].

Father Merolla, a still earlier traveller, mentions these charms from the Congo district (1682). The fourth abuse is that whilst their children are young these people bind them about with certain superstitious cords made by the wizards, who likewise teach them to utter a kind of spell while they are binding them. They also at the same time hang about them bones and teeth of divers animals, being preservatives, as they say, against the power of any disease.

Likewise, there are some mothers so foolish that they will hang Agnus Deis, medals, and relics to the aforesaid cords' [54, xvi. 237]. 'To remedy these disorders, we have thought proper to issue forth the following ordinances: That all mothers should make the cords they bound their infants with of palm leaves that had been consecrated on Palm Sunday; moreover guard them well with other such relics as we are accustomed to make use of at the time of baptism' [54, xvi. 239].

These fetish charms may be worshipped and regarded as anthropopathic, when they are true fetishes, or they may be merely 'lucky' with no religious regard or spiritual interpretation, or they may be anything between the two extremes.

7. Just as the human body and soul form one individual, so the material object and its occupying spirit or power form one individual, more vague perhaps, but still with many attributes distinctively human. It possesses personality and will, it has also many human characters. It possesses most of the human passions, anger, revenge, also generosity and gratitude; it is within reach of influence and may be benevolent, hence to be deprecated and placated, and its aid enlisted [53, 62].

The objects used as fetishes by the Ainu, sticks, skulls of animals, claws, paws, mistletoe, stones, etc., are all looked upon as animate, with a distinct life of their own, with power to protect their worshippers in time of danger, heal them when sick, and bless them with general prosperity [4, 375-6].

In this characteristic, in the possession of personality and will, in its material and spiritual duality, a fetish differs from a charm or an amulet as from an idol; it is always 'anthropopathic' [61, 61].

8. The fetish may act by will or force of its own proper spirit, or by force of a foreign spirit, entering or acting on it from without. 'Beyond the regularly recognized habitats of the spirits, that may be called natural to them, any other location may be acquired by them temporarily, for longer or shorter periods' [53, 62].

When the fetish acts by force of its own proper spirit, it is something more than mere Animism. It does not become a fetish by applying the general belief in souls to a special object, but by a process which has been divided by Schultze into four stages [62, 215-223]:

a. The value which an uncultured man attributes to any object is often exaggerated, especially if the object is in any way conspicuous, unusual, or mysterious.

b. He attributes to it an anthropopathic nature, believing that all natural objects are like man, with human characteristics.

c. By the causal connection of ideas he associates the object with auspicious or inauspicious events, which he believes it to influence.

d. A belief in its power leads him to reverence it, and to attempt to conciliate and propitiate the power by worship.

As an example, the anchor cast up on the beach at the mouth of the river Keissi [45] may be cited:

a. The anchor was an unusual object, and was therefore credited with an exaggerated value and regarded with great interest.

b. It was believed to possess a life of its own, a soul or spirit, somewhat analogous to man's.

c. A Kaffir broke off a piece of the anchor, and he soon afterwards died. The two events were associated with one another, and
the breaking of the anchor was believed to have caused the death.

d. The power of the anchor-spirit was thus established, and
the natives worshipped it in fear and hope.

Thus the fetish was evolved. But more commonly a spirit is
attracted to the object from without, as in the case of the *suhman* of
the Gold Coast, where the spirit of the Sasabonsum is invited into
the stone or other object prepared for it, or as in the most usual
type of West African fetish, where the wandering spirit becomes
localised in an object by means of the ceremonies and conjurings
of the Uganga or magic doctor [53, 81].

The distinction between the different powers animating the
fetish are clearly distinguishable on the Gold Coast [16, 275]. The Tshi
believe that everything in nature is animated; that everything not
made with hands has an indwelling spirit, possessing powers beneficial or prejudicial to man, according to whether it is propitiated
or neglected; so the more dangerous spirits, those of rivers, mountains, rocks, and shoals are worshipped. Later on an image is made
of the nature-god, from material from his habitat, and it is brought
to a place more convenient for the worshippers, and forms their
tutelary deity. Gradually his origin is forgotten, and the nature-god
becomes a fetish.

But besides these 'nature-gods' there are 'ghost-gods.' The
fetish may be animated by a ghost-god, for the power of dead men

lives on in their ghosts; sacrifices are made to them, and ghost-gods also develop into tutelary deities. Perhaps ancestor-worship and Fetishism may be more intimately related than is generally acknowledged [16, 280]. The Melanesians believe that the souls of the dead act through bones; while the independent spirits choose stones as their mediums [6, 131].

9. In the popular view of Fetishism the material object was worshipped in its own character, but one of the fundamental conceptions of the West African fetish is that the spirit and the material object can be dissociated, and that, although the spirit is temporarily incorporated in the fetish, yet the two are no more inseparable than man's soul and body. The conception of the duality of everything lies at the root of all the West African beliefs. 'Everything that he knows by means of his senses, he regards as a twofold entity—part spirit, part not spirit, or, as we should say, matter; the connection of a certain spirit with a certain mass of matter, he holds, is not permanent. He will point out to you a lightning-struck tree, and tell you it's spirit has been broken; he will tell you, when the cooking-pot has been broken, that it has lost its spirit; if his weapon fails, it is because someone has stolen, or made its spirit sick by witchcraft. In every action of his life he shows you how much he lives with a great powerful spirit world around him' [39, 141].

When the spirit is 'dead' the fetish has no further value, the little thing you kept the spirit in is no more use now, and only fit to sell to a white man as "a big curio"!' [40, 304-5]. But occasionally sanctity still clings to the former dwelling of the spirit, and it is used as a charm, though no longer worshipped as a fetish.

The *Mirrone*, a tree worshipped in the Congo region, was the tutelary god of the dwelling, and the owners placed calabashes full of palm-tree wine at the foot of the tree for the spirit to drink, 'nor do they dare to tread upon its leaves any more than we would on the holy cross.' But if it were damaged in any way, they no longer worshipped it, but they stripped off the bark or rind, which was made into petticoats for the women, to act as protecting charms [54, xvi. 236]. Owing to the possibility of the spirit leaving the fetish, it has to be tested, to see whether it really contains an indwelling spirit or no, and the natives of the Gold Coast put their Bohsum in the fire as a probation. If the fire injures it in the very least degree, it is not a true Bohsum, there is no indwelling spirit [15, 92].

Sometimes the spirit is forcibly ejected from his dwelling-place for a particular purpose. Soon after Sir Richard Burton had arrived at Dahome, a fetish youth made his appearance in the evening, knelt down before the domestic altar, broke some of the images, and went away declaring that he had called out the fetishes, and that I might after the evocatio deorum do my worst' [9, i. 299].

10. The fetish is *worshipped, prayed to, sacrificed to, and talked with*, as a sentient and willing personification of the spirit or power. Examples of sacrifices and prayers and worship offered to the fetishes are found in all parts, and many instances have already been quoted. Offerings of food and drink are placed before them daily, and sometimes a cock is sacrificed; occasionally, if the worshippers are rich, a sheep is killed, 'which they offer up to the gods

in words alone, for they immediately fall upon it and tear it to pieces with their fingers' *(54, xvi. 400)*.

The personal interest of the fetishes in the affairs of their worshippers is seen in the ceremonies connected with the death and burial of the Fiote. 'When all are assembled, the elder addresses the two family fetishes held by two of the family. Pointing and shaking his hand at them, he tells them how the deceased died, and all the family has done to settle the matter: he tells them how they have allowed the father to be taken, and prays them to protect the rest of the family; and when he has finished his address the two who hold the fetishes pick up a little earth and throw it on the heads of the fetishes, then, lifting them up, rub their heads in the earth in front of them' *(13, 135)*.

11. The fetish is petted or ill-treated with regard to its past or future behaviour. The spirit is invited to enter the suhman charm prepared for it by promises of offerings and food *(16, 100)*, and special offerings are made before embarking on any great enterprise.

But when conciliation fails, the owner sometimes has resort to force, though Colonel Ellis states that in all his experience of the natives of the Gold Coast he has never seen or heard of any coercion of a fetish by the natives, and that the idea of coercion is entirely foreign to their minds *(15, 194)*. The Kafirs appear to be harsher in their methods.

'The Caffres play at a game of chance before their idols, and, should chance be against them, kick and box their idols; but if, after this correction, on pursuing their experiments they should continue unsuccessful, they burn the hands and feet of them in the fire; should ill fortune still attend them, they cast the idols on the ground, tread them under foot, dash them about with such force as to break them to pieces. Some, indeed, who show greater veneration for the images, content themselves with fettering and binding them until they have obtained their end; but should this not take place as early as their impatience looks for, they fasten them to a cord and gradually let them down into the water, even to the bottom, thus trusting to force them to be propitious; if after this good fortune should not follow, the idols are then withdrawn from the water, the patience of even the milder Caffres becomes exhausted, and the images are subjected to the grossest indignations' [54, xvi. 696]. The negro in Guinea beats his fetish if his wishes are frustrated, and hides it in his waist cloth when he is about to do something of which he is ashamed' [38, 91].

III. Fetishism as a Form of Religious Worship

FETISHISM IS A stage of religious development associated with a low grade of consciousness and of civilization, and it forms a basis from which many other modes of religious thought have developed, so that it is difficult to point out where fetishism ends and nature-worship, ancestor- worship, totemism, polytheism, and idolatry begin, or to distinguish between a fetish, an idol, and a deity.

It includes conceptions which are purely magical, coercion of the supernatural by means of natural objects; and it also includes conceptions which persist into higher forms of religion, such as the worship of the symbol of an unseen power.

It is an early product of the primitive religious instinct of humanity, developing at a low grade of culture among a people of a highly imaginative temperament.

The fundamental religious feeling which is everywhere part of the mental equipment of man has been called by Marett supernaturalism, and is perhaps best indicated in English by the term awe, in which word are implicated fear, wonder, admiration, interest, respect, even love, perhaps. The object of this religious 'sense,' or, as many would call it, 'instinct,' is the supernatural. The recognition of the supernatural, the fundamental religious feeling of awe, develops in two ways. 'There arises in the region of human thought a powerful impulse to objectify, and even personify, the mysterious or 'supernatural' something felt; and in the region of will a corresponding impulse to render it innocuous, or, better still, propitious, by force of constraint, communion, or conciliation' [50, 168].

So man personifies the power which he cannot understand, calling it by names which we translate as spirit or god, and he worships it, propitiating and conciliating it by offerings and sacrifice, and entering into communion with it by prayer. Thus are produced the two fundamental factors of religion, the belief in some mysterious power, and the desire to enter into communication with the power by means of worship. The worship of different groups of peoples expresses itself in different ways, reflecting the mental type of the worshippers, their civilization, their culture, their character and temperament.

The cold, practical, phlegmatic Northerners worship within bare walls, while the fervour of the imaginative South demands expression in an elaborate ritual, with richness of decoration, warmth of colour, dim lights and soft music. The extraordinarily vivid imagination and the childlike capacity for 'make-believe' of the negro, lead him further still; the lively fancy of the West African demands a visible object to which worship may be directed. He wishes really and sensibly to behold and even to possess his god, so he incorporates him in a tangible object, and satisfies his religious ardour by directing his worship to that object. Thus fetishism and the fetish are evolved.

Bibliography

1. Allen, J. *Modern Judaism*. London: Hamilton, 1816.
2. Armit, W. E. *Customs of the Australian Aborigines*. Joum. Anth. Inst., ix. London, 1880.
3. Arnot, Fred. S. *Garenganze, or Seven Years' Pioneer Mission Work in Central Africa*. London: Hawkins, 1889.
4. Batchelor, J. *The Ainu and their Folk-Lore*. London: Religious Tract Society, 1901.
5. Bogoras, W. *The Chuckchee*. The Jessup North Pacific Expedition, vii. (1) Leiden: Brill; New York: Stachert, 1904.
6. Brinton, D. G. *The Religions of Primitive Peoples*. New York: Putnams, 1897.
7. *The Myths of the New World; a Treatise on the Symbolism and Mythology of the Red Race of America* (3rd Ed.) Philadelphia: M'Kay, 1896.
8. Brosses, Ch. de. *Du culte des dieux fetiches*. Paris: 1760.
9. Burton, R. F. *Mission to Gelcle, King of Dahome*. London: Tinsley Bros., 1864.
10. Casalis, E. *The Basutos, or Twenty-three Years in South Africa*. London: Nisbet & Co., 1861.
11. Clodd, E. *Tom Tit Tot; an Essay on Savage Philosophy in Folktale*. London: Duckworth, 1898.
12. Codrington, R. H. *The Melanesians: Studies in their Anthropology and Folk-Lore*. Oxford: Clarendon Press, 1891.
1 3. Dennett, R. E. *Death and Burial of the Fiote*. Folk-Lore, viii. 1897.
14. Dobrizhoffer, M. *An Account of the Abijwnes, an Equestrian People of Paraguay*. London: Murray, 1822.
15. Ellis, A. B. *The Tshi-speaking Peoples of the Gold Coast of West Africa*. London: Chapman & Hall, 1887.
16. *The Yoruba-speaking Peoples of the Slave Coast of West Africa*. London: Chapman & Hall, 1894.
17. Ellis, W. *Polynesian Researches*. London: Fisher, Son & Jackson (2nd Ed.), 1831.
18. Elworthy, F. T. *The Evil Eye*. London: Murray, 1895.
19. Fletcher, Alice C. *The Import of the Totem*. Report Am. Assoc. Advanc. Sci. (Detroit Meeting, 1897); also 'Notes,5 etc. (Buftalo Meeting, 1896).
20. Frazer, J. G. *The Golden Bough; a Study in Magic and Religion*. (2nd Eel.) London: Macmillan & Co., 1900.
21. *Lectures on the Early History of the Kingship*. London: Macmillan & Co., 1905.

22. Friedel, E. *Brandenburgia;* Monatsblatt der Gesellschaft fur Heimatkunde der Provinz Brandenburg, Berlin, xii. 1904.
23. Garner, It. 0. *Superstitions of the West African Tribes.* 5 Austral. Ass. Rep. 1895.
24. Gaster, M. *Two Thousand Years of a Charm against the Child-Stealing Witch.* 5 Folk-Lore, xi. 1900.
25. Gregory, Augusta, Lady. *Gods and Fighting Men.* London: Murray, 1904.
26. Gunn, Jeannie. *The Little Black Princess; a True Tale of Life in the Never-Never Land.* London: Moring, 1905.
27. Haudon, A. C. *The Study of Man.* London: Murray. 1898.
28. Haddon, A.C. Head Hunters; *Black, White, and Brown.* London: Methuen, 1901.
29. *Reports of the Cambridge Anthropological Expedition to Torres Straits.* Cambridge University Press, 1904.
30. Hartland, E. S. *The Legend of Ferseus; a Study of Tradition in Story, Custom, and Belief.* London: Nutt, 1894-6.
31. Hays, H. M. *Hypnotism, its History, Nature, and Use.* Pop. Sci. Monthly, lxvii. New York, 1905.
32. Hirn, Y. *The Origins of Art; a Psychological and Sociological Inquiry.* London: Macmillan & Co., 1900.
33. Holmes, J. *Notes on the Religious Ideas of the Elema Tribe of the Papuan Gulf.* Journ. Anth. Inst., xxxii. 1902.
34. Howitt, A. W. *On Australian Medicine Men.* Journ. Anth. Inst., xvi. London, 1886.
35. *The Native Tribes of South- East Australia.* London: Macmillan, 1904.
36. Jevons, P, B. *An Introduction to the History of Religion.* (2nd Ed.) London: Methuen & Co., 1902.
37. Joyce, P. W. *A Social History of Ancient Ireland.* London: Longmans, Green & Co., 1903.
38. Kidd, D. *The Essential Kafir.* London: Black, 1904.
39. Kingsley, M. H. *The Fetish View of the Human Soul.* Folk-Lore, viii. 1897.
40. *Travels in West Africa.* London: Macmillan, 1898.
41. *West African Studies.* London: Macmillan, 1899.
42. Lane, E. W. *Maimers and Customs of the Modern Egyptians.* Paisley and London: A. Gardner, 1895.
43. Leland, C. G. *Etruscan Roman Remains in Popular Tradition.* London: Fisher Unwin, 1892.
44. Letourneau, C. *La Sociologie.* Paris: Reinwald, 1880.
45. Lichtenstein, H. *Travels in Southern Africa.* London: Colburn, 1812.
46. Lippert, J. *Die Religionen cler Europaischen Culturvölker.* Berlin, 1881.

47. Luptonh 1000 *Notable Things.* 1612.
48. Macdonald, S. *Old World Survivals in Ross-shire.* Folk-Lore, xiv. 1903.
49. Maclagan, R. C. *Notes on Folk-lore Objects collected in Argyleshire.* Folk-Lore, vi. 1895.
50. Marett, R. R. *Pre-animistic Religion.* Folk-Lore, xi. 1900.
51. *From Spell to Prayer.* Folk-Lore, xv. 1904.
52. Max Muller, F. *Natural Religion.* London: Longmans, 1892.
53. Nassau, R. H. *Fetichism in West Africa.* London: Duckworth, 1904.
54. Pinkerton, J. *A General Collection of the Best and Most Interesting Voyages and Travels in all Parts of the World.* London: Longmans, 1814.
55. Podmore, F. *Apparitions and Thought-Transference.* London: W. Scott, 1894.
56. Owen, Mary A. *Folk-lore of the Musquakie Indians of North America.* London: Nutt, 1904.
57. *Old Rabbit the Voodoo and other Sorcerers.* London: T. Fisher Unwin, 1893.
58. Rhys, J. *Welsh Fairies.* Nineteenth Century, Oct. 1891.
59. Roth, H. Ling. *On the Significance of Comrade.* Journ. Anth. Inst., xxii. 1893.
60. *The Natives of Sarawak and British North Borneo.* London: Truelove & Hanson, 1896.
61. Saussaye, P. D. C. de la. *Manual of the Science of Religion.* London: Longmans, 1891.
62. Schultze, F. *Psychologie der Naturvölker.* Leipzig: Veit, 1900.
63. Skeat, W. W. *Malay Magic.* London: Macmillan, 1900.
64. Spencer, B., and Gillen, F. J. *The Native Tribes of Central Australia.* London: Macmillan, 1899.
65. St. John, S. *Life in the Forests of the Far Fast.* London: Smith, Elder & Co., 1862.
66. Stokes, Whitley. *The Destruction of Da Derga's Hostel.* Revue Celtique.
67. Super, C. W. *Physicians and Philosophers.* Pop. Science Monthly, lxvii. New York, 1905.
68. Swettenham, F. A. *Malay Sketches.* London: Lane, 1895.
69. Taylor, R. *Te Ika a Maui.* London: Macintosh, 1870.
70. Tylor, E. B. *Researches into the Early History of Mankind and the Development of Civilisation.* (3rd Ed.) London: Murray, 1878.
71. *Primitive Culture.* (2nd Ed.) London: Murray, 1873.
72. Westermarck, E. *The Magic Origin of Moorish Designs.* Journ. Anth. Inst., xxxiv. 1904. Printed by T. and A. Constable, Printers to His Majesty at the Edinburgh University Press

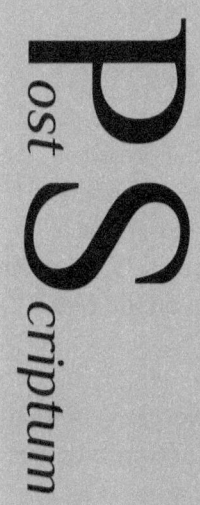

Indigenous
people
and the
importance
of securing
all possible
information

About Haddon

VAMzzz Publishing

Alfred Cort Haddon

The author

Alfred Cort Haddon, Sc.D., FRS, FRGS
(Finsbury, 24 May 1855 – 20 April 1940,
Cambridge) was an influential British
anthropologist and ethnologist. Initially a
biologist, who achieved his most notable
fieldwork, with W.H.R. Rivers, C.G. Seligman,
Sidney Ray, Anthony Wilkin on the Torres
Strait Islands.

Alfred C. Haddon was the eldest son of John
Haddon, the head of a firm of type-founders
and printers. He attended lectures at King's
College London before entering Christ's
College, Cambridge in 1875. At Cambridge,
he studied zoology. Shortly after attaining his
Master of Arts degree, Haddon was appointed
as Demonstrator in Zoology at Cambridge in
1882. For a time he studied marine biology in
Naples. In 1883 he was appointed Professor of
Zoology at the College of Science in Dublin.
The same year he got married. Among his
first publications were *An Introduction to
Embryology* in 1887, and various papers on
marine biology, which led to his being invited
to go to the Torres Strait Islands to study
coral reefs and marine zoology, and while
thus engaged he first became attracted to
anthropology.

On his return home, he published many
papers dealing with the indigenous people,
urging the importance of securing all possible

2

information about these and kindred peoples before they were overwhelmed by civilization. He advocated that in Cambridge (encouraged thereto by Thomas Henry Huxley), whither he came to give lectures at the Anatomy School from 1894 to 1898, and at last funds were raised to equip an expedition to the Torres Straits Islands to make a scientific study of the people, and Dr. Haddon was asked to assume the leadership.

In April 1898, the expedition arrived at its field of work and spent over a year in the Torres Strait Islands, and Borneo, and brought home a large collection of ethnographical specimens, some of which are now in the British Museum, but the bulk of them for one of the glories of the Museum of Archaeology and Anthropology, University of Cambridge. Haddon was convinced that the hundreds of art objects collected, had to be saved from almost certain destruction by the zealous Christian missionaries intent on obliterating the religious traditions and ceremonies of the native islanders. Film footage of ceremonial dances was also collected. His findings were published in his 1901 book *Head-hunters, Black, White and Brown*.

In 1894, on his return home from his second expedition, he was elected a Fellow of his College (Junior Fellow in 1901, Senior Fellow in 1904). Haddon was appointed Lecturer in Ethnology at the University of Cambridge in

'Haddon was appointed Lecturer in Ethnology at the University of Cambridge.'

1900, and Reader in 1909, a post from which he retired in 1926. He was appointed advisory curator to the Horniman Museum in London in 1901. Haddon paid a third visit to New Guinea in 1914, and returned during the First World War.

Accompanied by his daughter Kathleen (1888–1961), a zoologist, photographer and scholar of string-figures, the Haddons travelled along the Papuan coast from Daru to Aroma. While less discussed than his earlier work in the Torres Straits, this trip was influential in helping shape Haddon's later work on the distribution of material culture across New Guinea. The war effort had largely destroyed the study of Anthropology at the University, however, and Haddon went to France to work for the Y.M.C.A.. After the war he renewed his constant struggle to establish a sound School of Anthropology in Cambridge.

On his retirement Haddon was made honorary keeper of the rich collections from New Guinea which the Cambridge Museum possesses, and also wrote up the remaining parts of the Torres Straits Reports, which his busy teaching and administrative life had forced him to set aside.

Bibliography

- *Evolution in Art* (1895)
- *Section H. Anthropology* (1896)
- *An Introduction to Embryology* (1887)
- *Professor Flinders Petrie's Scheme of an Ethnological Store-House* (1897)
- *The Study of Man* (1898)
- *Permanent Skin Decoration* (1901)
- *Head-hunters, Black, White and Brown* (1901)
- *Leland Stanford Junior University. A Suggestion* (1902)
- *Magic and Fetishism* (1906)
- *The Races of Man* (1909)
- *The Wanderings of People* (1911)
- *An Ascent of the Snowy Mountains of New Guinea* (1913)
- *Eonthropus Dawsoni* (1913)

'Haddon was convinced that the hundreds of art objects collected, had to be saved from almost certain destruction by the zealous Christian missionaries intent on obliterating the religious traditions and ceremonies of the native islanders.'

VAMzzz Publishing

Paper books

VAMzzz Publishing is located in the very centre of old Amsterdam, in The Netherlands. Our publishing company creates high quality revised editions of five star occult, witchcraft, Gothic and esoteric classics, mostly written in the Fin de siècle-period and early 20th century.

As a publisher, we deeply respect the writer of any book we choose, so we join our forces (top level graphic design & thirty years of occult studies) to produce enchanting volumes which maximize the reading pleasure and inform, often with extra added information. In contrast to the current trend of digital screen addiction, we think, this variety of literature needs to be presented on paper. *No e-books, but real books!*

Apart from re-publications of valuable but forgotten books, we are also in the preparation of new publications on topics such as self-healing, magic, new astrology and more.

Previews of all books including a complete table of contents can be viewed on www.vamzzz.com. More books will be added to the list. Please visit our website regularly for the latest updates.

VAMzzz Publishing
P.O. Box 3340
1001 AC Amsterdam
The Netherlands
contactvamzzz@gmail.com
www.vamzzz.com

Recommended

PAN Magazine
by VAMzzz Publishing
Free Online
www.vamzzz.com/pan.html

In Greek religion and mythology, PAN, the companion of the nymphs, is the god of the wild, shepherds and flocks, wild mountains and rustic music. He has the hindquarters, legs and horns of a goat, in the same manner as a faun or satyr. He is also recognized as the god of fields, groves and wooded glens; connected to fertility, the joy of life itself and the season of spring.

Though a mortal god in antiquity and an underground witch-god in medieval times, the last decades PAN has become a patron of both modern occultism, Wicca, paganism and the green guerilla – enthroned again as the one and only God of the Earth and Nature. PAN is the vibe touching those who refuse to become part of a machine, and who remain loyal to Mother Nature, the visible and hidden one. Therefore PAN is the most suitable icon we could chose for this periodical.

The Banshee
A Ghost Hunter's Investigation
by Elliot O'Donnell
222 pages, Paperback, ISBN 9789492355232

The banshee is a mysterious female spirit in Irish folklore, who heralds the death of a family member, usually by shrieking or keening. The screeching sound is described as somewhere between the wail of a woman and the moan of an owl, a low singing or piercing loud and able to break glass. The banshee appears as an old hag or beautiful lady, but may also appear as a crow, stoat, hare and weasel - animals associated in Ireland with witchcraft.

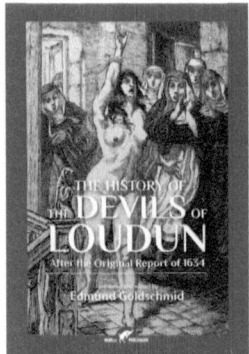

The History of the Devils of Loudun
After the Original Report of 1634
Translation by Edmund Goldschmid
118 pages, Paperback, ISBN 9789492355256

Around 1632 seventeen Ursuline Nuns were taken over by demons and went into a sexual and blasphemous state of hysteria for years. The work also describes the trial of a womanizing local priest named Father Urbain Grandier, who was accused of summoning these demons and, in the end, burned at the stake.

Religion and Lust
or The Physical Correlation of Religious Emotion and Sexual Desire
by James Weir Jr.
146 pages, Paperback, ISBN 9789492355270

In *Religion and Lust*, author James Weir Jr. investigates the origins of religious feeling, the once world wide spread fertility worship and the physical correlation of religious emotion and sexual desire. A major part of the work is filled with a colourful collection of religious or semi-religious, sexual rites, once practiced all over the globe, connecting the most "primitive" tribe to the most "civilized" nations.

Incubi and Succubi or Demoniality
A Historical Study of Sexual Contacts with Demons
by Sinistrari of Ameno
194 pages, Paperback, ISBN 9789492355263

This book is a revised English edition of Sinistrari's fascinating 17th century study on the orgasm-stimulating sex demon. The incubus and succubus are the same creature. The incubus is its male shape, copulates with women. The succubus visits men, triggering wet dreams. The intercourse with this astral visitor was called demoniality, a term no longer in use, though nowadays people are still having these mysterious incubus/succubus-"sexperiences".

Mysteria
History of the Secret Doctrines & Mystic Rites of Ancient Religions & Medieval and Modern Secret Orders
by Dr. Otto Henne am Rhyn
288 pages, Paperback, ISBN 9789492355225

Mysteria is a treasure box of missing conspiracy links and one of the very few publications, which offer reliable information about Adam Weishaupt's Illuminati for "the web & media-disinformed". Lodge-insider Otto Henne am Rhyn takes you on a journey, back to the Mystery cults of ancient Egypt, Babylon and Greece, passes Templars and explains modern lodges.

Magic and Magical Fetish
by Alfred Cort Haddon
108 pages, Paperback, ISBN 9789492355300

Alfred C. Haddon gives a practical and theoretical insight of the universal principles of magic, categorized in different techniques. The book is one of the very few works ever published, which describes wind and rain making. Magic is divided into sympathetic magic, the magic of words, talismans and divination, magical training routines. A kaleidoscope of forgotten magical techniques, which wasn't available for decades.

The Eleusian and Bacchic Mysteries
A Dissertation
by Thomas Taylor
200 pages, Paperback, ISBN 9789492355294

The Eleusian and Bacchic Mysteries focus on life, death and rebirth in a living nature (the present), while this nature was regarded as the converging of past and future. Taylor describes a series of lost secret rites. These rites were once the appointed means for regeneration through an inner union with the Divine Essence, despite their wild and sexual aspect.

Numbers
Their Occult Power and Mystic Virtues
by W. Wynn Westcott
170 pages, Paperback, ISBN 9789492355287

This book may be regarded as the "bible of numerology". It deals with Pythagorean number divisions, explains 3 different kinds of Kabalistic numerology, and reveals the hidden logic and symbolism of the numbers 1,2,3,4,5,6,7,8,9,10,11,12 and 13. This is accompanied by a long course of numbers between 14 and 25920. Special symbolisms are included like the link between numbers and planets and numbers in relation to the Apocalypse.

Sorceress
A Study of Witches and their Relations with Demons
by Jules Michelet
432 pages, Paperback, ISBN 9789492355249

This work is one of the most vivid, dark and confronting studies on witchcraft ever produced. Long before Murray's Witch-Cult in Western Europe, Michelet positions the medieval witch within a diminishing ancient culture of nature worship and the ruthless efforts of Christianity, with its cruel hostility towards nature, life (and women), to overwrite it. A nightmare of the most extraordinary verisimilitude and poetical power...

Aradia
Gospel of the Witches
by Charles Godfrey Leland
174 pages, Paperback, ISBN 9789492355010

This wonderful book describes the creation according to Italian witch-lore. We also read about the witch-meeting or sabbath (treguenda) and the book contains many original magical recipes, like spells for love and good fortune. Diana is further connected to the Moon and the fairy world.

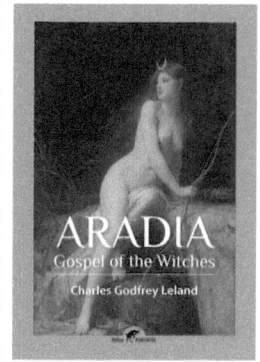

Demonology and Devil-Lore *(Volume 1)*
by Moncure Daniel Conway
490 pages, Paperback, ISBN 9789492355157

Demonology and Devil-Lore *(Volume 2)*
by Moncure Daniel Conway
518 pages, Paperback, ISBN 9789492355164

Within the demonology scope, this rare and mostly forgotten, almost 1000 pages thick masterpiece, remains unsurpassed in quality and completeness. Even in the 21st century the works offer fascinating missing links for both the academic and student of occult traditions. Moncure Daniel Conway divides Volume 1 in three parts and deals mainly with the evolution and thematic classification of ex-gods, demons and nature creatures. Volume 2 deals primarily with the diabolic and with the Devil himself, his ethnic history and connected topics.

Fairy Mythology (Volume 1)
Romance and Superstition of Various Countries 1
by Thomas Keightley
404 pages, Paperback, ISBN 9789492355096

Fairy Mythology (Volume 2)
Romance and Superstition of Various Countries 2
by Thomas Keightley
404 pages, Paperback, ISBN 9789492355102

The term Fairy covers all kinds of nature spirits, not just the tiny sugarsweet creatures hovering around flowers. A unique and impressive book on this subject, published in a revised 2 volume-edition. No wiccan or pagan can afford to leave these books unopened. About Elves, Dwarfs, Kobolds, Trolls, Changelings, Meremaids, Nisses, Fairies, Brownies, Puck and other Elemental spirits all over the world.

Etruscan Magic & Occult Remedies
(Two volumes in one book)
by Charles Godfrey Leland
628 pages, Paperback, ISBN 9789492355003

Part One of the book gives us a complete and detailed insight in the Etruscan and Roman rooted pantheon of the Tuscan Streghe (witches). Part Two describes many of their spells, incantations, sorcery and several lost divination methods. Much information in this book, Leland received first hand from the Tuscan witches Maddalena and Marietta.

Voodoos and Obeahs
Phases of West India Witchcraft
by Joseph J. Williams
374 pages, Paperback, ISBN 9789492355119

This work goes into great depth concerning the New World-African connection and is highly recommended if you want a deep understanding of the dramatic historical background of Haitian and Jamaican magic and witchcraft, and the profound influence of imperialism, slavery and racism on its development. Williams includes numerous quotations from rare documents and books on the topic.

Devil-worship in France
Or The Question of Lucifer
by Arthur Edward Waite
240 pages, Paperback, ISBN 9789492355065

In *Devil-Worship in France,* Waite attempts to discern what is genuine from what is fake in the evidence of 19th century Satanism. To get the answers he spends a great deal of time investigating the French Masonic echelon, debunking a "conspiracy of falsehood" and determining what should be understood by Satanism and what not. Huysmans' diabolical novel *Là-Bas* (1891) inspired Waite to write this sceptical analysis.

Testament of Solomon
A First Century AD Grimoire
76 pages, Paperback, ISBN 9789492355041

A first century AD grimoire, and therefore the oldest, and least known, of all grimoires (magical instruction books) in the occult tradition. The book describes health inflicting demons of zodiacal decans, summoned by King Solomon, and how he controlled them to use their forces to build his temple and more. Translated by F. C. Conybeare, appeared first in the *Jewish Quarterly Review* of October, 1898.

Ophiolatreia
Rites and Mysteries of Serpent Worship
by Hargrave Jennings
186 pages, Paperback, ISBN 9789492355126

An account of the rites and mysteries connected with the origin, rise and development of serpent worship in various parts of the world, enriched with interesting traditions, and a full description of the celebrated serpent mounds & temples, the whole forming an exposition of one of the phases of phallic, or sex worship.

Anansi
Jamaican stories of the Spider God
by Martha Warren Beckwith
494 pages, Paperback, ISBN 9789492355171

Anansi is both a god, spirit and African folktale character. He often takes the shape of a spider and is considered to be the spirit of all knowledge of stories. He is also one of the most important characters of West African and Caribbean folklore.

Spiritual Fetichism
A Study of West African Culture, Witchcraft, Magic & Demonology
by Robert Hamill Nassau
524 pages, Paperback, ISBN 9789492355188

Despite a nowadays anachronist and disturbing perspective, the book has remained most valuable for students of the occult, especially those interested in demonology, voodoo, hoodoo and its roots, African magick and religion, witchcraft, the classes of African spirits, and of course the spiritual and magickal use of a fetish.

Là-Bas
A Journey into the Self
by Joris-Karl Huysmans
378 pages, Paperback, ISBN 9789492355058

The plot of *Là-Bas* concerns the novelist Durtal, who is disgusted by the emptiness and vulgarity of the modern world. He seeks relief by turning to the study of the Middle Ages. Through his contacts in Paris, Durtal discovers that Satanism is not a thing of the past but alive and kicking in turn of the century France. The novel culminates with a description of a black mass.

Unicorn
A mythological investigation
by Robert Brown Jr.
124 pages, Paperback, ISBN 9789492355072

Brown Jr. believes the unicorn to be a lunar symbol, and draws on mythology from a wide range of sources all over the world to build his case. The author discusses the heraldic use of the unicorn, relates the creature to ancient goddesses like Astarte, Hecate en the Gorgon Medusa, and provides the reader with lost esoteric Moon-lore.

The House of Souls
A Fragment of Life / The White People
The Great God Pan / The Inmost Light
by Arthur Machen
336 pages, Paperback, ISBN 9789492355218

A collection of four masterpieces of horror and mystery, first collectively published in 1906. In the ingenious plot of *The Great God Pan,* a young woman is forced into Pan's reality, and turns into a femme fatale. *The Inmost Light* involves a doctor's scientific experiments into occultism and a vampiric force. In *The White People* a young girl's diary is discovered, describing her initiation into a secret world of folklore and ritual magic. In *A Fragment of Life* Machen tries to convince us of a hidden reality.

Taboo, Magic, Spirits
A study of primitive elements in Roman religion
by Eli Edward Burriss
200 pages, Paperback, ISBN 9789492355034

In Ancient Rome Mana was the term used for a mysterious, magical medium, which could be helpful or harmful (Taboo). Just like the Chinese qi, it could empower the positive and the negative. Contents: Mana, Magic and Animism – Positive and Negative Mana (Taboo) – Miscellaneous Taboos – Magic Acts: The General Principles – Removing Evils by - Magic Acts – Incantation and Prayer– Naturalism and Animism.

Chaldean Magic
It's Origin and Development
by François Lenormant
454 pages, Paperback, ISBN 9789492355027

The essentials of magic in Chaldea are presented inside a context of comparison or contrast to Egyptian, Median, Turanian, Finno-Tartarian and Akkadian magic, mythologies, religion and speech. Interesting is the Chaldean demonology, with its incubus, succubus, vampire, nightmare and many Elemental spirits, most of them coalesced with the primal powers of nature.

Amazons - *Two publications in one book -*
I. *The Amazons* by Guy Cadogan Rothery
II. *Religious Cults Associated With the Amazons*
   by Florence Mary Bennett
328 pages, Paperback, ISBN 9789492355089

Contents I: The Amazons of Antiquity – Amazons in Far Asia – Modern Amazons of the Caucasus – Amazons of Europe – Amazons of Africa – Amazons of America – The Amazon Stones. Contents II: The Amazons in Greek legend – The Great Mother – Ephesian Artemis – Artemis Astrateia and Apollo Amazonius – Ares.